Wakefield Press

West–Eastern Divan

The WEST–EASTERN DIVAN of JOHANN WOLFGANG VON GOETHE

translated from the German by
ROBERT MARTIN

Wakefield
Press

Wakefield Press
16 Rose Street
Mile End
South Australia 5031
www.wakefieldpress.com.au

First published 2016

Translation copyright © Robert Martin, 2016

All rights reserved. This book is copyright. Apart from any
fair dealing for the purposes of private study, research,
criticism or review, as permitted under the Copyright Act,
no part may be reproduced without written permission.
Enquiries should be addressed to the publisher.

Cover designed by Liz Nicholson, designBITE
Text designed and typeset by Wakefield Press

National Library of Australia Cataloguing-in-Publication entry

Creator:	Goethe, Johann Wolfgang von, 1749–1832, author.
Title:	The West–Eastern divan of Johann Wolfgang von Goethe / Johann Wolfgang von Goethe; translated by Robert Martin.
ISBN:	978 1 74305 423 9 (paperback).
Subjects:	German poetry – Translations into English.
Other Creators/Contributors:	Martin, Robert, translator.
Dewey Number:	831.6

This translation is for

Patricia June Sumerling

'So fallen meine Lieder
Gehäuft in deinen Schoss.'

and Matthew Montaigne

'Geliebter Knabe,
Bleibe jung und bleibe klug.'

'Den geretteten Schatz
Für ewig zu sichern,
Teilt ich ihn weislich
Zwischen Suleika und Saki.'

Contents

Translator's Preface	ix
MOGANNI NAMEH	
Book of the Singer	1
HAFIS NAMEH	
Book of Hafez	23
USCHK NAMEH	
Book of Love	35
TEFKIR NAMEH	
Book of Reflections	49
RENDSCH NAMEH	
Book of Displeasure	63
HIKMET NAMEH	
Book of Proverbs	77
TIMUR NAMEH	
Book of Timur	87
SULEIKA NAMEH	
Book of Suleika	91
SAKI NAMEH	
Book of the Cupbearer	129
MATHAL NAMEH	
Book of Parables	143
PARSI NAMEH	
Book of the Parsee	149
CHULD NAMEH	
Book of Paradise	155
A selection from the unpublished poems	175
Glossary	183

Translator's Preface

In 1814, when Goethe was in his mid-sixties, a double inspiration began to work upon him. He read a translation of Hafez, one of the great poets of Persia, and he fell in love with a young, talented and beautiful woman named Marianne. The result was the *West–oestlicher Divan*, a cycle of poems first published in 1819. I have translated the version of 1827, the second and final edition to come from Goethe's hand. It was his intention to further expand the collection, and I have added a selection from the poems left unpublished at his death.

A few of the poems in the *Divan* were written by Marianne herself. Goethe gave her the name 'Suleika', and called himself 'Hatem' – elsewhere he is simply 'the Poet'.

When Goethe began the *Divan*, he had already published much poetry, drama, and prose, including *Werther*, *Iphigenie*, the first part of *Wilhelm Meister*, and the first part of *Faust*. He had served for decades in many administrative and artistic roles at the court of the Duchy of Weimar in central Germany, and had undertaken research in various fields of science.

In Hafez, Goethe found a kindred spirit, a poet from four and a half centuries earlier who, like him, saw God at work in the beautiful, the creative, and the loving, and who chafed at the power of the orthodox and small-minded. In his own *Divan* Goethe, often playfully, adopted and adapted various conventions, images, ideas and language from Hafez, and from other writers in Persian, Arabic and Turkish.

And during a nostalgic journey to the Rhineland, he

made the acquaintance of Marianne Jung, a young actress in the care, and soon to be the wife, of his friend Johann Jakob von Willemer. Of the many women that Goethe conceived a passion for, Marianne was intellectually and artistically the most accomplished. Although their times together were brief, and soon ended, they exchanged letters and poetry till Goethe's death in 1832. Only many years later did Marianne von Willemer reveal that she was 'Suleika', and that she had written a handful of the poems in the *Divan*.

In my translation I have tried to approximate the metrical patterns of the originals, but made no attempts at rhyme. I shall not labour the point that translation involves many kinds of compromise and loss.

I have not sought to burden the text with learned notes, but the reader will find some explanatory remarks in a glossary at the end of the volume.

May this translation contribute to the World Literature that Goethe called for. And in this time of conflict and anxiety, such as he knew during the Revolutionary and Napoleonic Wars, may the translation contribute to understanding between the West and the world of Islam. As the poet himself says:

> Seeing others like ourselves,
> We become aware that
> What are known as West and East
> Cannot be untangled.
>
> Movement back and forth between the
> Worlds is what I here approve of:
> Thus to range the lengths of East and
> West declares the highest wisdom!

TRANSLATOR'S PREFACE

The *Divan*, abundant in forms and moods, declares the universality, the common humanity, of a yearning for love, delight, youthfulness, enrichment of life, and ultimately transcendence – whether in Persia or Europe, the Middle Ages or the modern era.

Robert Martin
Adelaide, South Australia, 2016

MOGANNI NAMEH

Book of the Singer

In the decades that are gone,
I enjoyed a share of pleasures;
Strung in handsome cavalcade,
Like the golden days of Baghdad.

Hegira

North and West and South are fractured,
Thrones exploding, empires quaking;
Fly out East where things are clearer,
Taste an air that's patriarchal:
What with loving, drinking, singing,
Khizer's well shall make you younger.

There in regions pure and righteous
I shall plumb the human species'
Deepest origins, to ages
When they still received from God the
Lore of Heaven in common speech, their
Heads not cracked by such instruction.

High respect they paid their fathers,
Shunning servitude with strangers;
I'll enjoy a younger, bounded
World, with narrow thought but wider
Faith, and words of greater value
For the words are spoken only.

I'll associate with shepherds,
Seek refreshment at oases,
Wander on with caravans while
Trading shawls and musk and coffee;
I'll step out on every pathway
From the deserts to the cities.

BOOK OF THE SINGER

Hafez, in the dangers of the
Rocky trail, your songs warm up the
Heart, while fits of rapture seize our
Guide: he's singing from the lofty
Saddle of his mule, to rouse the
Stars and frighten off the bandits.

Then I'll follow your example,
Sainted Hafez, when at watering
Spots and taverns, girlfriends lift their
Veils and shake perfume from loosened
Ringlets – Yes! the poet's whispered
Love could wake desire in houris.

If you envy this or even
Long to spoil a thing for someone,
Know the poet's words are at the
Gates of Paradise forever
Hovering and gently knocking,
Praying there for life eternal.

Pledges

Talismans, when they've been wrought
From cornelian, bring us luck;
Should an onyx be their mounting,
Dedicate to them some kisses!
Driving evil from the door,
Guarding you, your home as well,
If engraved with pure and plain
Words that sound the names of Allah,
They inspire your love and striving.
Women gain a special blessing
From the talisman's protection.

Amulets are much the same, with
Symbols written out on paper;
Here, though, there is less restriction
Than in handling precious stones, and
So devoted souls may choose a
Longer verse, if they prefer it.
Faithful people then enclose them
In a scapular's embrace.

Inscriptions have no hidden extra bits,
They are themselves, and should give all the meaning;
Whatever else you honestly would like to
Append, they cry: 'It's said! It's done!'

BOOK OF THE SINGER

I would seldom choose Abraxas!
Often just a grotesque image
Dreamed up by a solemn fool, and
Claiming great significance – so
If I mouth absurdities, just
Think, he's giving me Abraxas.

A signet ring is hard to fashion:
The deepest wish in narrow space;
But if you know it's truly dedicated,
The word is as engraved, you let it stand.

Free Spirit

Leave me be, I only love the saddle!
You can stay there in your tents and shanties!
I'll be riding briskly to the farthest
Points, with nought but stars above my headgear.

For you He set the stars in their place
To lead you by land and sea,
To give you endless happiness
In gazing at the heights.

BOOK OF THE SINGER

Talismans

Eastern lands belong to God!
Western lands belong to God!
All the peoples of the earth do
Know the peace of His embracing.

———————

He, exclusively the Righteous,
Wills to each a just provision.
May of all His hundred names be
This, amen, the highest honoured!

———————

In my erring is confusion;
But Thou knowest to unbind me.
In my deeds and in my sayings,
Grant Thou me a straightened pathway!

———————

My imaginings are worldly,
Yet to richer harvestings do win me;
Not disbanded with the dust, the spirit
Striveth in itself and striveth higher.

———————

Within thy breathings are blessings united:
To take in air, and then to unburden;
That doth constrain, this doth refresh;
In wondrous form thine existence was mixed.
Thank thou the Lord when He doth press,
And thank Him when He doth grant a release.

Four Favours

The Arabs in their wandering
Can cross the world in gladness,
Since Allah gave them for their share
A quartet of His favours.

The turban first, a better trim
Than any kingly headgear;
A tent, to move from spot to spot,
So home is where the tent is.

A sword, a fitter guardian
Than cliff or city walling;
A song, that pleases and has use
In setting traps for women.

The flowers from her shawl fall down
Defenceless to my music;
She knows quite well it's all for her,
And ever is obliging.

With fruit and flowers I can set
A dainty table for you;
And should you want a yarn as well,
I'll spin you one that's novel.

Confession

What is hard of concealment? A fire is!
In the daytime betrayed by smoke,
By night revealed as a flaming demon.
Harder to hide the passion of love:
No matter how encasing the mask,
It signals itself with timid eyes.
A poem's the hardest yet to suppress:
No bushel's known can hide this light.
On tossing off a new production,
The poet's quite infatuated,
Writes out a neat and careful draft, and
Angles for universal homage.
He's pleased as Punch and reads to all
Aloud, to bore, and edify.

Raw Materials

Just what subject matters are there
For a worthwhile song to draw on,
That a layman will enjoy and
Connoisseurs can hear with pleasure?

Love above all other matters
Is the topic fit for singing;
When a song is driven by it,
Words and tune are all the better.

Then the sound of glasses clinking
With a wine that burns like rubies:
It's the lovers and the drinkers
Who can sport the brightest garlands.

Sound of arms is also fitting,
When a trumpet's blaring loudly;
So, when Fortune blazes flames, a
Hero's victory makes him godlike.

Then at last, and quite essential,
That the poet – who loves beauty –
Also knows the way to hate, to
Hate what's ugly and what's shameful.

When the singer knows the handling
Of these four primeval powers,
Then, like Hafez, he can always
Please and animate his listeners.

To Create and Animate

From just a dumpling made of dirt,
The Lord had fashioned Adam;
And since his mother was the Earth,
He lacked sophistication.

Through Adam's nose the Elohim
Then puffed the means of thinking;
What help this was he showed at once
By sharp allergic symptoms.

With member, head, and skeleton,
He still was just a dumpling,
Till Noah found the tankard fit
For alcohol's reception.

The dumpling felt an inward leap,
The day he wet his whistle,
As sure as yeast supplies to dough
The requisite ignition.

So, Hafez, your congenial songs,
And sanctified example,
With clink of glasses lead us up
To Our Creator's dwelling.

Phenomenon

Phoebus and clouds of rain
Couple together,
Making an arcing rim
Shaded with colour.

In mists the god again
Draws out a circle;
Arcs then are painted white –
Still arcs of heaven.

So should you, green if grey,
Not feel afflicted;
White showing through the hair
Won't kill the passion.

BOOK OF THE SINGER

Loveliness

What's the varied colour there, that
Binds the heights and sky together?
Morning mists are dazzling to my
Normal clarity of vision.

Are they awnings the Vizier has
Set up for his cherished women?
Are they carpets for the feasting
As he weds his current favourite?

Red and white, arrayed at random,
I don't know a sight more lovely;
Hafez, could Shiraz your city
Reach this gloomy Northern province?

Yes, they are a crowd of poppies,
Spread like motley throngs of neighbours
And, to mock the god of war, they
Deck the fields with cheerful bunting.

May the kindly skittish creatures
Always use such ornament, and
May the sun shine, as today, to
Light them brightly on my journey!

Discord

Close by the riverbank
Cupid is fluting,
Mars on the other side
Blows at his trumpet.
Flute to the gentle ear
Wafts an enticement,
That's till the bloom of song's
Rubbed off by clamour.
Now flute contends against
Loud warlike thunder;
I grow distracted, mad –
Does that surprise you?
Shrill grow the fluted notes,
Booms the tromboning;
I rage and rush about –
Is that a wonder?

BOOK OF THE SINGER

The Past in the Present

Roses, lilies, damp with morning,
Flourish in a nearby garden;
Shading them, benign and wooded,
Rocky slopes mount up to heaven;
Fringed with giant trees, its crown a
Mediaeval fort, the mountain
Circles round until it falls to
Reconcilement with the valley.

And the breeze is redolent of
Days when love afflicted us, when
Notes from my guitar contended
With the gleaming rays of sunrise;
Times when hunting parties shouted
Robust music from the forests,
Now arousing, now reviving,
As a heart desired or needed.

Ceaseless growth within the forest
Should encourage you to learn that
What you in your time encountered,
It can now be felt through others.
None can then allege against us
Envy of another's pleasure;
So at every stage of life be
Well-prepared for what is offered.

Singing thus, again we meet with
Hafez; and it's fit that we should
Bring the day to its perfection
In enjoyment with an adept.

Song and Form

Let the Greek dragoon his clay
Firmly into sculpture,
Massing up with both his hands
Joy at his creation.

Here for us there's wonderment
Grasping our Euphrates,
Letting fingers play amongst
Freely flowing liquid.

When this cools my burning soul,
Songs fly out unprompted;
Drawn when poets' hands are cleansed,
Water is self-shaping.

Boldness

Overall the most secure way
Strength and health are anchored?
No one can resist a full tone,
Sound that's huge and vibrant.

See that nothing checks the athlete!
Have no dull ambition!
Songs insist – just like the CV –
Poets do some living.

Live to make the shout of bronze bells
Clamour through your spirit!
Poets, though they feel the heart quake,
Reach themselves to wholeness.

Fit and Able

Poems spring from cockiness,
Don't you shake your head!
Why don't you ignite the blood,
Free and brisk like me?

If my life were full of care,
With a bitter taste,
I'd be unassuming, yes,
Even more than you.

Modesty's a pretty thing
For a growing girl:
She'll be won by tenderness,
Not by pushy brutes.

And I'd take the humble path
With the worthy sage
Who could explicate for me
Universe and Time.

Poems spring from cockiness!
Don't be turned aside.
Boys and girls with fiery blood,
You could come along!

Little monk with naked head,
Stop your tiresome yack!
Sure, you'd make an end of me –
As for humble, no!

BOOK OF THE SINGER

Preaching empty sentences
Does no good at all;
That's a shoe that's had its sole
Worn away before.

When the poet's millwheel turns,
It just can't be stopped:
Those who've understood our ways,
They'll forgive as well.

A Universal Stirring

Dust's among the stock-in-trade that
You manipulate adroitly,
Hafez, when to praise a lover,
You compose a pretty lyric.

Then the dust upon her threshold's
More appealing than a carpet
Worked in gold-embroidered flowers,
Kneeled upon by Mahmud's minions.

When the wind across her doorway
Drives the clouds of dust so briskly,
More than musk you love the fragrance,
Better than the oil of roses.

Dust's a thing I've long been missing
In the foggy Northern regions;
Now the heated South has furnished
Quite enough to satisfy me.

For so long the door I worship
Rests unmoved upon its hinges!
Send a thunderstorm and rain to
Heal me with the smell of greenness!

When the thunderclouds are rolling,
All of heaven flashes lightning,
From the wind the moisture gathers
Savage dust and bears its earthward.

Then at once an animation
Swells a secret holy process,
And it's green itself, and greening
Of the world that circumscribes us.

Blessed Yearning

Don't tell people, only wise ones,
While the mob will jeer at wisdom,
I intend to praise the creatures
That are burning for extinction.

In the cool of loving nights, that
Once conceived you, now engage you,
Strange awareness seizes on you
While the silent candle glistens.

There's an end to your confinement
In the shadows, in the darkness,
As new longings tear you upward
To engender higher being.

Distance cannot make you weary,
You are flown along in trance
Till, you moth, the light you ache for
Brings the death you seek in flame.

Till you take this for your goal:
Growth that seems like dying!
You are just a shadowed guest
On a darkened planet.

Sugarcane comes forth to bring
Sweetness to the people!
May the outflow from my pen
Ever be engaging!

HAFIS NAMEH

Book of Hafez

Let the Word be named the Bride,
Spirit be the Groom;
Theirs a marriage known to those
Grasping Hafez' worth.

Soubriquet

Poet
Muhammad Shamsuddin, why would
They give you, your worthy people,
Hafez for a name?

Hafez
                I value,
And will answer, your enquiry:
Since I joyfully preserve the
Solemn legacy, committed
Word for word, of Islam's Holy
Book, conducting myself meekly,
So that common daily troubles
Do not reach to me or them, and
Cherishing the Prophet's words and
Offspring, as is right and proper –
Therefore they gave me the title.

Poet
Hafez, then, it seems to me that
I should never leave your side, for
When our thoughts are like another's,
We in general grow together.
And I match you so completely,
That our Holy Bible's glorious
Words are my secure possession –
Just as on that Cloth of Cloths the
Likeness of Our Lord was printed –
Stirring in my quiet breast, in
Spite of doubters, hindrance, losses,
Images of bright conviction.

Accusation

Do you know then whom the devils watch for
In the desert, haunting cliffs and hillsides?
Waiting for an opportunity to
Capture them and haul them to damnation?
They watch out for liars and for rogues.

Why then does the poet not avoid
Company with people of this nature!

Can't he see through those he hangs around with?
He whose only merchandise is madness?
Lacking self-control, he's driven through the
Wilds by an obsession with romance, and
Writes complaining verses in the sand, that
Breezes chase away at once;
Unaware of what he says,
What he says, he can't live up to.

But his songs, they always get a hearing,
Though they contradict the Holy Book.
Teach us then, you that are canon lawyers,
Wise ones, pious, deeply learned, keep us
Faithful Muslims dutiful and strict.

Hafez often gives especial grounds for scandal,
Sprinkles doubts and worry in our spirits:
Tell us, what reaction is expected?

Fatwa

Hafez has recorded in his writings
Truths that cannot be erased or countered;
Here and there, however, trifling matters
Stray beyond the law's determined limits.
If you'd safely go, you must distinguish
Serpent's venom from its antidote – and
So the wisest course by far, averting
Downfall, lies in your submission with a
Cheerful courage to the joy of noble
Actions, guarding yourself wisely from errors,
Such as promise only eternal sorrow.
Thus has written wretched Ebusuud.
God forgive him all his wealth of sinning!

BOOK OF HAFEZ

The German Gives Thanks

Holiest Ebusuud, you have hit it!
Such a sainted man the poet hopes for;
For precisely when those trifling matters
Stray beyond the law's determined limits,
That's his nature, when in soaring spirits,
He finds pleasure even in his troubles.
Serpent's venom, antidote, to
Him they must appear as like each other.
That one does not kill, nor this one cure him:
For the valid life consists in acts of
Lasting blamelessness, in that they prove that
Any harm done, falls upon their author.
Therefore can the ancient poet hope that
He, transfigured to a youth, shall know the
Welcome that the houris give in Heaven.
Holiest Ebusuud, you have hit it!

Fatwa

The Mufti read the poems of Mizri,
One then another, all were examined,
Till soberly he threw them in the furnace;
Exquisite volume, all reduced to nothing.

Send those for burning, spake the lofty justice,
Who speak and think like Mizri – he alone
The pain of death by burning should be spared:
For Allah gave each poet his potential.
Should he abuse it by his sinning, leave him
To settle his accounts direct with Allah.

Unbounded

That you can never end, that makes you vast,
And never will begin, that is your fate.
Your song is turning like the starry heavens,
End and beginning endlessly each other,
And what the centre holds, is visibly
That which at last remains and first appeared.

You are the spring of true poetic pleasure,
As wave on wave unnumbered from you rises.
A mouth forever set to kiss,
A song profound and sweetly flowing,
A throat that always thirsts for wine,
A spirit of abundant kindness.

I'll let the world go wholly under,
Hafez, with you, with you alone
I'll try my mettle! Pleasure, pain –
Let's share experience as twins!
To rival you in loving, drinking,
Shall be my pride, and fill my life.

My song, now sound in turn your passion!
With older, younger, voice than Hafez.

Imitation

I hope to find myself within your verses,
And simple repetitions bring me pleasure,
First get the meaning, then I find the wording;
I shall not sound a sound a second instance,
Unless it give the meaning special grounding,
As you can do, most favoured of the poets!

The way a clever spark, to set on fire the
Imperial city, fanning furious flames up,
Engenders winds from any likely breezes,
Itself expiring, dead in halls of stardom:
So your undying ardour leaps from you, to
Arouse a German heart with fresh excitement.

Predetermined rhythms do bring pleasure,
Talent gives itself much joy therein:
But how quickly they become repulsive,
Hollow masks that lack in blood and brain.
There's no sign of gladness in a spirit
Which, concerned with novel forms, has not
Rid itself of forms that are defunct.

Open Secret

They've labelled you, holiest Hafez,
The 'mystical tongue', but not grasped,
These babbling man-dictionaries,
The worth conveyed in your words.

Mystics you could call *them*, when
They attribute to you their folly,
And pour out their impure wine
From bottles bearing your label.

You rather are mystic pure,
Since it's way past their grasp
That you, lacking godliness, have been blessed!
That's something they're not keen to concede.

Hint

And yet they've got it right, those I censure:
Since words have more than single meaning,
That's something people can find themselves.
A word is a fan! Eluding the sticks, the
Glance of a duo of beautiful eyes.
The fan, well it's just a delicate gauze
Which, although it cover the face,
Fails in its aim to disguise the girl,
Since the best of her ornaments,
Her eyes, emit electric flash.

To Hafez

What all are seeking, you perceived
With strengthened understanding:
From dust to throne, desire enchains
Us all in heavy harness.

It brings us pain, and yet such joy,
Who tries to thwart its power?
And though one gets a broken neck,
The next one keeps his courage.

Forgive me, Master, as you know,
I'm often past my limits,
When she, a roaming cypress tree,
Draws after her my glances.

Like drifting cypress-roots her feet
Caress the earth beneath her;
Her greeting melts like gentle clouds,
Her breath is loving zephyrs.

A weird sensation presses us
As ringlets curl and ripple,
In dark abundance welling up
While breezes purr among them.

And when she turns her open brow,
Its brightness calms the spirit,
Inspiring songs of joy and truth
That give the soul refreshment.

And now her lips are moving with
An action that's so charming:
At once they set your spirit free,
And bear you down in shackles.

BOOK OF HAFEZ

Your breathing comes in painful gasps,
As soul to soul is flying,
A fragrance winds its way in bliss,
Unseen in clouds of longing.

So when almighty passion burns
You reach out for the bottle:
The serving boy runs to and fro,
With one drink, then another.

His eyes are bright, his heart astir,
He hopes for your instruction,
To hear you in your highest flights,
As wine exalts your reason.

The cosmos opens up to him,
Within come grace and order,
His breast expands, he sprouts a beard,
And grows to young adulthood.

And when no secret's held from you,
In world and human nature,
You give the faithful student just
The hint to bloom his spirit.

And what we're due from princely gold
Shall not go wanting to us:
You grant the Shah a timely word
And pass it to the Vizier.

All this you know, and sing today,
And sing again tomorrow:
Your friendly guidance sees us through
The rough and smooth of living.

USCHK NAMEH

Book of Love

Tell to me
What my heart desires?

My heart is with you,
Hold it dear.

Paragons

Hear and be mindful:
Six pairs of lovers.
Description kindles, passion blazes:
Rustam and Tamina.
Unaware how near they stand:
Joseph and Suleika.
Yearning, denied their reward:
Farhad and Shirin.
Each other's only love:
Majnun and Layla.
Loving when youth is past:
Jamil and Buteina.
Sweet the games of lovers:
Solomon and his Sheba!
Keeping these well in mind,
You are strengthened in love.

One Pair More

Yes, loving brings a great reward!
Who gains a handsomer return?
You won't know power, won't get rich,
Yet equal any hero's worth.
And just as men recall the Prophet,
They'll speak of Wamik and his Asra.
But there's no story, just the names: and
The names are known to all and sundry.
What they achieved, what they endured,
No one recalls! That they did love,
That's all we know. Enough in that
When Wamik, Asra, are brought to mind.

A Reader

Strangest book of all, the Book of
Books, the Book of Love, which
I have read attentively, its
Pages sparse with joy, and
Sorrow filling tomes; a
Section just for separation.
On reunion, one fragmented
Little chapter! Pain in volumes,
Lengthened out by exegesis,
Endless, lacking bounds.
But Nizami! you perceived the
Proper way to resolution.
The insoluble, who solve it?
Lovers in return to union.

Yes, the eyes and mouth had full effect,
With their glances, and its kisses.
Rounded body, slender hips,
Matching Paradise in pleasures.
Was she real? Where is she now?
Yes! she was, she gave herself, she
Gave herself to me an hour,
And enchained me for a lifetime.

Warned

I as well was much too pleased,
Tangled in their tresses,
And so, Hafez, this your friend
Knew the same adventures.

But it's fashion now to wear
Lengthy hair in plaits, and
Fence with helmets on their heads –
We learn all about it.

Those who give it careful thought,
They resist compulsion:
People shy at heavy chains,
Lighter snares they run to.

Preoccupied

So round a head, so rich in curls! –
When I'm allowed to fill my hands with such an
Exuberance of hair and let them wander,
I'm filled with deep contentment in my heart.
I kiss the forehead, eyebrows, eyes and mouth,
And always know a freshness and a wound.
The combing hand, where should it end its journey? –
Again returning to the ringlets.
The ear does not evade the game,
This is not flesh, this is not skin,
So light in play, so full of love!
The man who strokes this little head
Will run his hands about forever
In such an affluence of ringlets.
So have you, Hafez, also done,
We do it from the start again.

Precarious

Shall I preach of emeralds your
Finger sets off gracefully?
Frequently a word's required, but
Often better left unsaid.

This I'll tell you, that the colour's
Green and pleasing to the eye!
Do not say there's cause to fear the
Pain and scars that wait at hand.

Nonetheless! you could uncover
Why you use this power to hurt!
'In your being there is danger,
Just as jewels bring delight.'

Oh my dear! in stubborn bindings
Freest songs are held constrained, that
Once in clearest lands of heaven
Flew about with life and lightness.
Time brings everything to ruin,
These alone preserve themselves!
Every line shall be immortal,
Live, with love, eternally.

Cold Comfort

Tears and sobs racked me while I
Longed for you at midnight.
The ghosts of darkness drew near,
And I was ashamed.
'Ghosts of darkness', I said,
'Sobbing and crying
You do find me, that you once
Passed as he reclined in sleep.
I am missing a great good.
Think no evil of me,
That you once called a wise man;
Heavy troubles befell him!'
And the ghosts of darkness,
With sombre expressions,
Made their way past,
Quite uncaring whether I be
Wise or imbecilic.

Easily Satisfied

'A fantasist you are,
Believing it's love that has brought you the girl.
There's something that I just can't stomach:
In flattery she's well experienced.'

Poet
I'm quite contented that I get it!
What serves me for excuse is this:
Love is voluntarily given,
Flattery is my due.

Greeting

O how favoured am I!
I wander lands where
The Hudhud crosses my pathway.
I sought in rocks the fossils
Of ancient oceans of molluscs;
Hudhud ran about,
Unfolding his crown in
Strutting and mocking display,
Liveliest creature joking
Over dead ones.
'Hudhud', said I, 'it's true!
A handsome birdy you are.
Hurry now, Hoopoe Bird!
Hurry with a message
To my sweetheart, promise her
That I'm hers forever.
For Solomon
Once, you flew out to
The Queen of Sheba as
Go-between by royal command!'

Resignation

You perish yet are so cheerful,
You pine but your song is sweet?

Poet
In hatefulness love has been dealing!
Happily I concede
I sing with a heavy spirit.
But look upon the candles:
They shine as they're wasting away.

Pain of love reviewed the available
Sites of loneness and desolation;
It found at last my empty heart
And nestled itself in the vacuum.

Unavoidable

Who can give orders for silence,
When the birds flock the fields?
Who can forbid from its struggles
A sheep enduring the shears?

Does it seem I am unruly,
When they assault my fleece?
No! The wild behaviour is forced by
The shearer who holds me down.

Who will forbid me from singing
Out loud to clouds up on high,
Confiding to the heavens
How she made me fall in love?

Secret

All who see them stand amazed at
Glances from my darling's eyes, yet
I alone am in the secret,
Know quite well the hidden meaning.

For they mean: I cherish this one,
And not that one, or another.
Leave it off, you charming people,
With your gapes and wishful thinking!

Yes, with terrifying power,
All around she fires her glances:
But she only seeks to flash him
Sweetest cues for assignations.

Most Secret

'We are anxious to discover,
We, the hunters after gossip,
Who your girlfriend is, and whether
You have rivals for her favour.

'You are smitten, we can see it –
We are pleased to compliment you;
But that she could love you back, is
Something we just cannot credit.'

Feel at ease, respected Sirs, and
Seek her out! But pay attention:
When you see her, you'll be staggered,
When she's gone, you'll kiss the aura.

You know how Shihabuddin
Dropped his cloak on Arafat; do
You call a man a fool for
Acting in a similar manner?

When in presence of the Sultan
Or before the All-Beloved,
If your name is only spoken,
No reward can lift you higher.

Therefore once the dying Majnun,
He endured his greatest sorrow,
Whilst entreating that his name should
Not be mentioned to his Layla.

TEFKIR NAMEH

Book of Reflections

Hear the advice that the lyre proclaims;
It will help if you're equal to the song.
The happiest words will suffer scorn
If the audience lacks the ear.

'The lyre's song, what is it?' It sings aloud:
The fairest, she is not the finest bride;
But should we desire you be counted with us,
Aspire to the beautiful, seek perfection.

Five Things

Five things from which another five don't grow;
To this instruction open up your ears:
No friendship springs within a haughty spirit;
No manners in companionship with scoundrels;
An evil man cannot attain distinction;
The envious do not regard the needy;
The liar hopes in vain for trust and credence;
Hold fast to this, let no one steal it from you.

Five Others

What for me shortens time?
Active life!
What makes it drag to hateful length?
Idleness!
What makes a debtor?
Patience with burdens!
What brings reward in?
No lengthy debating!
How be respected?
Be armoured!

Fetching is a girl's expression, hinting;
Drinkers' looks are fetching, when expectant;
Condescending greetings from the master;
Autumn sun that brings you warmth and blessing.
Lovelier than all of these within your
Sight however, when a needy hand is
Prettily advancing for your gift, and
Sweetly thankful, what you give, receiving.
What a glance! a welcome! speaking longing!
See it right, and you'll be ever giving.

All that's in the Book of Pand
Lies inscribed on your own heart, for
When you give with your own will,
You love others as yourself; so
Blithely distribute your wealth,
Pile up no bequest of gold, and
Hurry gladly to prefer
Present times before nostalgia.

Riding on your way beside a smith,
Who knows, what day he'll shoe your horse;
Seeing humble cottage in open fields,
Who knows, could it tend the girl for you?
Happen meet with a soldier boy, brave and fair,
In future combat he kills you, or you kill him.
A vineyard is likely to give you reason
To claim it is bound to yield some value.
Thus you are sent, to life entrusted;
The balance I shall not go on rehearsing.

Respect the greetings strangers give to you!
They're worth as much as greetings from a friend.
A word or two and then you say goodbye!
Your path is East and his is to the West –
If after many intervening years
You meet abruptly, gladly you exclaim:
It's him! and yes, the place! as though had not
So many ranging days by sea and land,
So many turning suns ensued between.
Now barter merchandise and share rewards!
An old entrustment works an added tie –
The first address is worth a thousand more;
So give a fond salute to all you meet.

They have always had a lot to
Say about your faults,
And to prove what they were saying,
Taken lots of care.
Would that they had named your virtues,
Told them like a friend,
Shown with loyal knowing whispers
How to choose the best;
Yet it's true, the very best is
Not concealed from me,
Which indeed can seldom add a
Novice to its cell.
Now at last a chosen pupil,
I receive the good
Taught by other people when their
Faults bring on regrets!

Bookfairs call you in to buy,
But with knowledge you distend.
Those who calmly view the world,
Learn how love can educate.
Be you day and night in motion,
Catching much and much acquiring,
Hearken at another doorway,
How to gather fitting knowledge.
If the right you're seeking for,
Know in God what makes for right;
Those who burn with purest love,
Gain a loving God's regard.

I was so principled,
And went without,
Which did for many years
Torture my soul;
Well thought of, and yet not,
What could it promise?
Then I tried sinning,
Set to with vigour;
Vice did not suit me though,
Tore me in pieces.
So I thought: principled
Still is the better,
Though it bring poverty,
Yet it's a bastion.

Do not ask which was the gate that
Let you into God's domain, but
Rather stay in calm and quiet
Where you found your own position.

Search around then for the wisest;
Take your orders from the mighty;
Those will give you good instruction,
These will steel your deeds and power.

If you, mild and faithful, render
Lengthy service to the public,
Know that there are none to hate you,
While the many come to love you.

Princes recognize the faithful,
They ensure a scope for action;
Then the new can prove itself as
Fit to stand with ancient practice.

My origins? That's still an open question,
My pathway here, that's hardly known to me,
But here and now in days of godlike gladness,
Like friends together joy and sorrow meet.
Oh sweet delight, when both have been united!
Alone, who would be laughing, who'd be crying?

Each takes his turn to step the path
And brings the rest behind him;
So let us journey swift and brave
And bold in life's adventure.
It holds you up, with sideways looks,
To gather heaps of flowers;
But nothing checks you quite as stern
As when you've been false-hearted.

Forbearance in handling your women!
A crooked rib is what she was made from,
Lord God Himself could not make her straighter.
You try to bend her, she breaks;
Leave her alone, and she gets more crooked;
My Honest Adam, which seems more painful? –
Forbearance in handling your women:
It can't be good to suffer a broken rib.

Our lives are just a rotten joke,
We lack for this and lack for that,
We seek too little, or too much,
And might and fortune play their part.
And should misfortune join the game,
None are then keen to shoulder loads.
But heirs at last are pleased to carry
Sir Can-Not, Will-Not in his coffin.

Our lives are just a silly game:
The further you go forward,
The sooner you achieve a goal
You'd rather not remain at.

They'll say, don't be a stupid goose;
But do not heed such people:
For now and then they'll glance around,
And tell you to go backward.

That's not the way the world is run,
Where all is straining forward;
When any trip or take a fall,
Do the others look behind them?

'The years have taken, so you say, an armful:
Authentic pleasure in the play of senses;
Recall of even favourite diversions
Is passing; touring through the broadest
Regions avails you nought; nor praise from betters,
Acknowledged ornament to honour – once it
Was true delight. Achievements no more stream for
You satisfaction, now you lack the spirit!
I do not know, what's left that you can speak of?'

Enough remains! The mind and heart are steadfast!

From initiates take counsel,
More secure in every instance!
When you struggle with a problem,
They know straight where you are lacking;
Likewise you may hope for plaudits
When they know that you've succeeded.

Openhanded, reap betrayal,
Tight-fisted, reap despoiling;
When sensible, led to confusion,
When rational, stretched to nothing;
Severe, they circumvent you,
Naive, they take you captive.
Be master of their falsehoods:
Deceived, become deceptive!

Those who hold command will praise, and
Then another time they'll censure,
These are things a faithful servant
Should assess at equal value.

Then they praise you for a trifle,
Censure where they ought to honour;
But should you remain forbearing,
You at last are well rewarded.

Let it be the same with Allah,
For the mighty and the little:
Act or suffer as is needed,
Still remain a willing servant.

BOOK OF REFLECTIONS

Shah Sadshan and His Ilk

Through all the din of foes
Beyond the Oxus,
Our song emboldened struts
The line you order!
There's nought to cause us fear,
Our lives are shielded:
Long lengthened be your days,
Your rule enduring!

Highest Favour

Uncontrolled, as I was then,
I acquired a gentle master;
It was later that I, tamed,
Found as well a gentle mistress.
They have spared me no demand,
Yet have always found me faithful,
Guarding me with tender care
As a treasure they discovered.
No one with two masters finds
He has reason to be happy;
Master, mistress, though, are pleased
They together found a Goethe,
And my star and fortune shine,
Since I found this noble couple.

Ferdausi speaks

O world! malicious and hardened you are!
You feed us, instruct us, and kill us alike.
Only the favoured of Allah is fed,
Instructed, alive and with riches and all.

What then makes riches? An enlivening sunshine
Brings cheer to the beggar as much as to others!
But there's no great call for the rich to be troubled
By beggars' unholy delight in their squalor.

Jalaluddin Rumi speaks

You linger in the world, it flies like dreams,
You journey, and a fate decides how far;
The day, if hot or cold, was never of your choosing,
What blooms for you, it straightway starts to wither.

Suleika speaks

The mirror says I have good looks!
You say that age will be my fate as well.
Eternal we shall stand in God:
Love Him in me this single blink in time.

RENDSCH NAMEH

Book of Displeasure

'Where did you come by fortune?
How could you be so favoured?
In rubbish-heaps of living,
How did you find the tinder
That's yet again reviving
Belated incandescence!'

You need not get your hopes up,
The sparks are not for sharing –
In distances unmeasured,
The heavens' starry ocean,
I never lost direction,
I often found renewal.

The sheep in waves of whiteness
Arrayed across the hillsides,
Concern to earnest shepherds,
Who share a humble supper,
These inoffensive people
That always gave me pleasure.

In terrifying darkness,
Beset by threats of warfare,
The groaning of the camels
Assaulted ear and spirit,
With foolish men that rode them
Impelled to shouts and swagger.

Forever passing onward,
Forever spreading wider,
With all that made enchantment
Eternally receding,
Blue, haunting desert armies,
A stripe of lying waters.

BOOK OF DISPLEASURE

Not a rhymester you will find that
Does not think he is the best, and
Not a fiddler but he'd rather
Scrape the tunes of his own making.

Me, I cannot criticize them;
When we give another honour,
We ourselves can only lessen.
Can we live, if others flourish?

That's precisely how I found it
In a certain antechamber:
Would they have the sense to tell a
Rodent turd from coriander?

They despised the out-of-fashion,
All these lively avant-garde, and
Flat refused to give respect to
Anyone of former greatness.

And where nations are divided,
And reciprocate their loathing,
Neither camp will recognize how
Like they are in their objectives.

And ill-mannered self-importance
Earns the censure of those people
Who themselves cannot abide that
Someone else gets any notice.

No sooner he's made a fist of his life,
A man's under threat from neighbours;
To see the capable man perform,
Drives them to wish him a stoning.
Then when, later on, he has died,
They rush to amass donations,
To honour his beleaguered life
By setting up a statue;
And yet the mob should undertake
To seek their best advantage:
A wiser deal would be to see
The man forgot forever.

BOOK OF DISPLEASURE

Eminence, you recognize it,
Always it will spring up somewhere;
I enjoy a conversation
With an expert or a tyrant.

Since the fools and narrow-minded
Ever made the loudest noises,
While the limited and half-wit
Tried to keep us subjugated,

I declared myself unshackled
From the foolish and the knowing,
When the latter have no feelings
And the former go to pieces.

Thinking power, love at last would
Force me back to union with them,
Threw the sun for me in shadows,
Made the shadows burn with fever.

Hafez too, and Ulrich Hutten,
Had to firmly gird themselves to
Combat rivals wearing habits;
Mine are dressed like any Christian.

'Tell us then who works against you!'
I shall name no individuals,
Since already in this parish
There's enough for me to bear with.

If you dwell upon the good,
I can never blame you;
If you even *do* some good,
See, it brings you honour!
If you'd rather draw a fence
Round the goods you're blest with,
I live free and dare to live
Free of all delusions.

For the people, they are good,
Would be better still if
In their actions they were not
Pushed around by others.
On the road, a saying's heard,
No one's like to censure:
Since we seek a common goal,
Let us walk together.

Many things will here and there
Set us at each other:
As a lover no one wants
Helpers or companions;
Gold and honours we prefer
Granted us uniquely;
And the wine, a faithful friend,
Brings at last division.

Over nonsense just like this
Hafez made pronouncements,
Over stupid tricks of life
Often cracked his noddle;
Then I don't see what it serves,
Running from existence,
Just as well, if worst has come,
Fix to tear your hair out.

BOOK OF DISPLEASURE

You would think a *name* could foster
Things that bud and bloom in silence!
Me, I love the fair and good that
Shape themselves from Allah's being.

I love someone, that is needful;
None I hate, unless it's called for:
Then as well I'm ready, willing,
Hate at once a whole department.

If you wish to know these better,
Study justice, study evil;
What *they* title excellent is
Probably a substitution.

Since to grasp authentic justice,
You must live from deep within you,
Sanctimonious preaching, meanwhile,
Seems to me a shallow labour.

Yes, the precious one can join up
With the one who splits a hair, and
Then at last the blusterer can
Think himself the best in judgement!

Daily each is only seeking
Novelty that's ever newer,
Till this very same diversion
Wrecks them in their inmost being.

This the toilers wish for, treasure,
Never mind what name *they* go by;
Yet a secret poem chirrups:
'Thus it was and ever shall be.'

Majnun then – I would not say that
He was altogether mad, and
You should not commence proceedings
Just because I say I'm Majnun.

When the heart, with candour brimming,
Vents itself, for your salvation,
Do not cry: 'Behold the madman!
Bring the rope and forge a shackle!'

When at last you see the prophet
Languishing in iron fetters,
It shall scorch you like a nettle,
Helpless gazing on that image.

BOOK OF DISPLEASURE

Did I ever seek to tell you
How to lead the troops in combat?
Did I criticize your actions,
If you then desired a treaty?

And I also left the fisher
Peaceful as he cast his net, and
Saw no need to take the skilful
Joiner's tools and make them sharper.

You however know it better,
More than I do, what my thought is,
All that Nature, zealous for me,
Made to be my own possession.

Do you feel an equal power?
Well, get on with your employments!
But on viewing my creations,
Note this first: that's how he willed them.

The Wanderer's Peace of Mind

What's the use deploring the
Cheap and low and banal,
For its might's gargantuan,
Let who will deny it.

Ruling through the vicious, it
Gains a high reward, with
Justice made a mockery by
Self-absorbed ambitions.

Nomad! could you hope to end
Such a deal of trouble?
Whirling winds of dried-up muck,
Let them spin to powder.

Why be asking from the world the
Things itself it misses, dreams of,
Glancing backwards, glancing sideways,
Wasting life in daily doses?
All endeavours, good intentions,
Limp behind the rush of life and
Then, what years ago you needed,
Now, today, the world may give you!

BOOK OF DISPLEASURE

To praise yourself declares a weakness,
Yet all who do some good are guilty here;
And if they in their words are not dissembling,
The good they *have* done rests a good.

So leave alone, you fools, the pleasure
Of one who sees himself as wise,
As he, a fool like you, misuses
The people's doubtful gratitude.

You believe that word of mouth
Makes for honest benefit?
Your tradition, O you gull:
Just a web of fantasy!
Judgement's first to shoulder arms;
From the chains of your religion
True salvation lies in reason,
Which you martyred long ago.

Whether gabbling French or English,
Or Italian – even German –
Each demands, just like the other,
What his love of self has prompted.

So they give no recognition,
Not in groups and singly neither,
If it doesn't foster promptly
What they see as their advantage.

Justice waits until tomorrow
For a friendlier reception,
While today the bad and wretched
Win the best of place and favour.

He that cannot give himself a
Lucid view of three millennia,
Rests in darkness, stays a novice,
Leads a day-by-day existence.

Once, when people quoted from the Koran, they
Cited you the chapter, and verse as well,
Which left a Muslim, as only proper,
Satisfied his conscience earnt respect and peace.
Today's fanatics are really no better,
They chatter the old, and they chatter the new.
The disorder grows daily greater.
O Holiest Scripture! O lasting repose!

BOOK OF DISPLEASURE

The Prophet speaks

One who's angered that it pleases God to
Grant Muhammad His protection, joy,
Let him find the hallway's strongest rafter,
Fixing to it then a sturdy rope,
Knot himself thereon! It holds and bears;
He will notice how his rage subsides.

Timur speaks

What? You're condemning of a mighty gale
Of arrogance, dishonest preachers?
If Allah wanted me a worm,
Then as a worm I'd be created.

HIKMET NAMEH

Book of Proverbs

I shall scatter talismans throughout the volume,
Winning equilibrium.
Those who use a pin with faith,
Everywhere they'll find a word that gladdens.

From present days, from present nights,
Demand no more
Than was on former days conveyed.

One who's born in the blackest epoch,
The blackest days will humour him somehow.

How light it can be,
Knows he that has made it, the one who achieved.

The sea flows forever,
The land can never keep it.

Why does the hour come laden with care? –
For life, it is brief, and days are long.
My heart, it's always yearning out,
But I don't know if heavenwards,
Prefers to wander to and fro,
And longs for freedom from itself;
On flying to the lover's breast,
It sleeps in heaven unaware;
When life then circles it away,
It hankers for a stable place;
What it may want, what it may lose,
It stays at last itself – a fool.

BOOK OF PROVERBS

Destiny tests you, know the reason why:
It aims at your forbearance: Hear! Obey!

Still is it day, the man exerts himself!
The night comes on, when none can go to work.

Why worry at the world? It's made and entire,
The Lord Creator has thought it all out.
Your lot is decided, submit to conditions,
The way is embarked on, accomplish the journey:
Your cares and your sorrows will change not a bit,
But fling you forever from equable stance.

When dejected people cry:
Help and hope are out of view,
There is still a healing power
Tendered in a friendly word.

'How maladroit then was your behaviour,
When Lady Luck had deigned a visit!'
The lady did not take it so badly
And more than a few times entered my household.

My birthright is splendid, wide and broad!
For time is my estate, my field to plough is time.

Do a good purely from love of goodness!
And hand this on to all your kind,
And should it not engage your children,
Your children's children get some good.

Anwari said, magnificent example,
That knew the deepest hearts and wisest spirits:
To gain in any place, at any time,
Be straight, discerning, ready to be pleased.

Why whine about opponents?
Could they ever become companions,
Seeing your nature, how you are,
Is permanent silent reproach to them?

Sillier's not to be suffered
Than when halfwits say to the experts
How they should, in days of greatness,
Prove to be humble in their manners.

If God so poor a neighbour were as
I can be and you can be,
We'd both be lacking in our credit;
He leaves every being as it is.

Confess! the oriental poets
Are greater than we of places west.
In one respect though we stand as their equals,
And that's in hatred of our rivals.

Everyone would like his fifteen minutes,
The way the world has been arranged.
Surely each can make a noise, but
Keep it to the things he understands.

BOOK OF PROVERBS

Spare us O God with Thy displeasure!
Wrens' utterances gain in volume.

Should an envy seek for trouble,
Let it feed upon its hunger.

Just to make sure you're respected,
Groom well your bristly hide.
Rabbits they hunt with falcons,
But not a feral pig.

What help are parsons' rulings
That only skew my path?
A thing not seized on when straight offered,
Is no more grasped if bent.

Praise of heroes, and broadcast of their names, will
Delight those that boldly fought themselves.
A person's worth you cannot discover
Till you yourself have endured extremes.

Do a good purely from love of goodness!
What you do does not reside,
And even if it remains, it
Will not stay your children's goods.

So none can rob, humiliate and shame you,
Conceal your gold, your plans, and your convictions.

How come, wherever we are going,
We're told much that is good, much inane?
The youngest keep rehearsing the words of the oldest,
And thinking that it all belongs to them.

Never let yourself be led
On paths of contradiction!
Sages tumble into ignorance,
Quarrelling with ignorant rivals.

'Why is the truth so far away?
Hiding below in deepest caverns?'
Who understands at fitting times!
When you at fitting times have grasped it,
Then is the truth akin and clear,
Entirely likeable and gentle.

Why would you set about to
Discern where kindness flows!
Just cast your bread on the waters;
Who knows who gets to eat!

One day, when I had extinguished a spider,
I paused: Was that a thing well done?
Had God for him, like me, ordained
An allotment of this existence!

'Darkness rules the night, the light's with God.
And why did He not grant us an equal boon?'

BOOK OF PROVERBS

What an assorted assembly!
With friends and foes at Our Maker's table.

You label me a stingy man;
Give me the goods to throw away!

Wanting me to show the prospect,
First you must ascend the rooftop.

The mute have little to fret for;
The tongue forever disguises the person.

A master is not well served
Who keeps two servants on.
A house in which two women live
Will not be cleanly swept.

You gentle people, be at peace
And just say 'God has spoken!'
And why persist with 'man and wife'?
It's Adam, Eve forever.

For what my highest thanks? – that Allah
Kept affliction and knowledge apart.
A patient has to sink despairing,
Who knows of illness what the doctor knows.

Foolish, that each one in his condition,
Prizes his own interpreting!
If Islam means we yield to God,
Then all are living and dying in Islam.

He comes to live life, builds a modern house,
He dies and leaves it to another,
Who changes it to suit himself, and
New work will never cease.

Guest in my house, he may be hard on
What I through years have tolerated;
By the door though he must be passing,
When it's *him* I cannot now put up with.

Lord, may you be pleased by
Such a little house!
Bigger can be built, but
Nothing more comes out.

Always secure as a haven
That no one seizes from you,
Two friends that bring no trouble:
Wine goblet, book of poems.

'What could not Lokman bring to pass,
That people saw as grim!'
The sweetness does not lie in canes:
The sugar, that is sweet.

Eastern lands in majesty
Made their way across the waters;
Friends of Hafez, they alone
Know what Calderon was singing.

BOOK OF PROVERBS

'What do you mean by adorned left hand,
Much more that can be fitting?'
What would a hand be called to do,
But complement its companion?

Should you send as Mecca pilgrim,
Jesus' donkey, you'd not find
Benefit to come thereby:
He would simply stay a donkey.

The trodden quark
Spreads out, gives way.
Should you though pound it with a will,
It takes a shape, a solid form.
Comparable brick you're well aware of,
Europeans call it a pisé.

Be not concerned, you worthy people,
Who does not fall, knows well where others stumble;
Alone the failure gets it right at once:
He knows then clearly how it's rightly done.

'So many you forgot to thank,
That gave you much of profit and value!'
For this neglect I'm not unsound,
And the gifts are living in my spirit.

Gain an honest reputation,
Practise competent discernment;
Seeking more than this, corrupts.

The sea of passion vainly storms and rages
Against the fixed, unconquered coast. —
It throws poetical pearls upon the shore,
And that is sure reward for living.

Confidant
You granted such a lot of requests,
And even when they caused you harm;
The worthy man now has asked for a scrap,
A thing that could not harbour a threat.

Vizier
The worthy man has asked for a scrap,
And had I granted his request,
He'd straightway be a defeated man.

It is bad, and looks very bad,
When truth will seek error's company;
But that is often her amusement;
How can we question her, so fetching?
However, should Master Error embrace her,
Miss Truth will find she is greatly ruffled.

I am much displeased, you know,
By this crowd of singers and talkers!
Who's driving poetry from the world?
                    Modern poets!

TIMUR NAMEH

Book of Timur

The Winter and Timur

So did Winter then surround them
In his mighty fury. Casting
Icy breath at every soldier,
He unleashed a pack of hateful
Winds to set upon the host.
All delivered to the mercy
Of his frosty-daggered tempests,
He descends on Timur's council,
Cries at him in words of menace:
'Venture slowly, wretched creature,
Gently, you unrighteous tyrant!
Shall your flames go on with searing,
Burning up the human spirit?
Are you numbered with accursed
Beings? well, I am another!
Old you are, and I! together
We afflict the land and people.
You are Mars! and I am Saturn,
Pair of evildoing planets,
In conjunction hideous.
You destroy a soul, congeal an
Atmosphere; and yet my winds are
Colder still than you may hope for.
Though your brutal army plunge the
Faithful in a thousand tortures,
Grant it God! that I endure to
See you reap a greater evil.
And by God, I'll help you nought.
Hear O God, my gift for Timur!

Yes by God! from mortal coldness
May you not be given aid by
Open hearths of glowing coal, nor
Flames of welcome in December.'

To Suleika

To caress you with a fragrance,
So your pleasure will augment,
First a thousand budding roses
Must endure a killing heat.

To obtain a single phial
That preserves the dear perfume,
Narrow like your finger's ending –
This demands a murdered world;

Yes, a world of urgent longing,
Whose desire for crowded life,
Nightingales in love portended
In their soul-disturbing song.

Should we suffer as they suffer,
When they amplify our joy?
Has not Timur's domination
Fed on multitudes of souls?

SULEIKA NAMEH

Book of Suleika

I imagined in the night,
I saw the moon enter my sleep;
When, however, I wakened,
The unpredicted – the sun – arose.

Invitation

Do not flee the present moment:
For the day to which you hurry
Is no better than today is;
But if you should stay contented –
Here where I have pushed away the
World, to draw a world towards me –
You and I will here have shelter.
Now is now, the morning morning,
And what comes and what is passing
Tugs us not and does not linger.
Just you stay my All-Beloved:
Then you bring all, and you give all.

That Suleika was taken with Joseph
Is no surprise:
He was young, youth is a boon,
He was beautiful, they say – to die for –
So was she, each to delight in the other.
But when it's you – you that I so long have hoped for –
Glancing to me your passion and youth,
Loving me, and promising joy,
This shall my poems keep on praising:
You are always to me Suleika.

BOOK OF SULEIKA

Now that you are called Suleika,
I as well should have a name.
When you celebrate your beloved,
Hatem's the name to give to me!
Only so there's something to be known by,
There's no presumption aimed at here:
Now Saint George's Knights, by such a title,
Don't claim Saint George as who they are.
Not Hatem Tai, not the ever-generous,
Can I in my privation be;
Hatem Tograi no, the richest living of
The host of poets – out of range:
Yet to keep the pair of these in my vision
Would not be altogether bad;
In taking, in giving the gifts of fortune,
There'll always reside a great content,
And feasting each other on loving
Will be a joy of Paradise.

Hatem

It's not chance that favours thieves, for
Luck's itself the greatest thief;
Now it's stolen what remaining
Love had lingered in my heart.

To you chance has handed over
All the profit of my life,
So that now my life is you, and
You alone I wait upon.

Yet already I see pity
In the jewel of your glance,
And delight that in your arms my
Fortune takes a better turn.

Suleika*

High delight in your affection
Means I cannot censure chance;
If it played the thief with you, the
Theft was such a joy to me!

And why think of it as robbing?
Give yourself by willing choice;
I'd be happy to believe I'd
Stolen you with my own hands.

What so freely you have given
Brings magnificent reward:
Riches of my life, my peace, I
Give them gladly, take them all!

Do not joke! Don't think privation!
Doesn't loving make us rich?
When you're held in my embraces,
There's no fortune passes mine.

* *Written by Marianne.*

BOOK OF SULEIKA

A lover is not soon turned aside,
No matter how the way is clouded.
Fetching Layla and Majnun back to life,
My leadership would set them straight in loving.

How comes it that I touch you, my darling,
And think of the gods when I hear your voice!
What chance of explaining the roses,
And accounting for nightingales?

Suleika

I was sailing on Euphrates:
From my finger slipped the gold
Ring you lately gave me, fell in
Gulfs of water, disappeared.

So I dreamed it. Morning's redness
Struck my eyelids through the trees.
Tell me, poet, tell me, prophet!
Give a meaning for this dream!

Hatem

I am willing to interpret!
Did I not before relate,
How the Doge of Venice takes the
Adriatic for his bride?

So the ring from Darling's finger
In Euphrates' waters fell.
Ah, to endless songs of heaven
I am stirred, engaging dream!

I, that roamed from Hindustan to
Reach Damascus in the West,
Journeyed then with caravans to
Farthest shores of Araby,

You have wed me to your river,
To the terrace, to this grove,
Here until the last embraces,
All my spirit vowed to you.

BOOK OF SULEIKA

Knowing well the looks that men are
Prone to give: 'I love, I suffer!
I am yearning, yes, despairing!' –
What the rest is, girls remember –
All of which cannot avail me,
All of which no longer moves me;
Come, however, Hatem's glances,
Straight the day begins to shine,
They affirming: 'She delights me,
As no other thing delights me.
Seeing roses, seeing lilies,
Any garden's trim and glory;
Myrtles, cypress, humble flowers,
Ever keen to add adornment;
She herself, adorned, is wonder;
Then embracing me, confounding,
She inspirits, heals and blesses,
Till I feel restored and whole and
Yet desire again to sicken.'
When you gazed on your Suleika,
Felt a healing in your sickness,
Felt a sickness in your healing,
Sent the smiles in my direction,
That you never smiled at others,
Then Suleika knew the glances'
Lasting message: 'She delights me,
As no other thing delights me.'

Ginkgo Biloba

Such a tree's leaf, now entrusted
From the East to my backyard,
Holds uplifting secret meanings
That initiates can taste.

Are there single living creatures
That divide themselves in two?
Are they two that choose to couple
So the semblance is they're one?

To unravel such enigmas,
I have found the proper guide:
Aren't you conscious that my poems
Show I'm one and double too?

Suleika

You have written many poems,
Aiming song in all directions,
From your hand exquisite script in
Splendid binding, golden edging,
T's all crossed and i's all dotted,
Nice enticements, book on book.
Yet they went, wherever turned, to
Promise you were true in love?

Hatem

Yes, the strong and favoured glances,
With enchantment in their smiles and
Teeth as well of dazzling white,
Needle-lashes, serpent-tresses,
Throat and bosom hung with magic,
Countless dangers in that place!
Think how long you were prefigured,
My Suleika, in those loves.

Suleika

The sun appears! A dazzling presence!
Enfolded by the sickle moon.
Who could be bonding such a couple?
This marvel, how explain it? how?

Hatem

The Sultan had the gift to marry
This highest pair of other worlds,
To designate the utmost-favoured,
The boldest in his loyal throng.

And let it symbolize our rapture!
Again I witness me and you:
Your sun is what you name me, Darling,
Come, sweetest moon, encircle me!

Come, Darling, come! and wind the headgear on me!
Your hand alone can make the turban fair.
And Abbas then, in Persia's highest station,
His apex was not tied with finer cloth!

A turban was the binding Alexander
Displayed in loops to deck his head,
And all ensuing rulers, all the others,
Took pleasure in the regal trim.

A turban also decorates the Kaiser;
It's called a crown, but any name will do!
The pearl and jewels! let the eye be ravished!
The fairest fabric still is mousseline.

And this example, pure and striped with silver,
O wind it, Darling, all around my brow.
What makes a ruler? That's not hard to answer!
Beneath your gaze, my stature is a king's.

BOOK OF SULEIKA

It isn't hard to keep me happy,
For I'm so willing to be pleased,
And sure the world has been obliging,
In giving me, well, not a lot!

I sit contented in the tavern,
Contented in my narrow house;
Yet think of you, and straight my spirit
Embarks on rout and overthrow.

The realms of Timur should attend you,
Obey you his submissive hosts,
And Badakshan be tolled for rubies,
With turquoise from the Caspian Sea;

For fruits, glacéed and honey-sweetened,
Bokhara, where the sun is bright,
With reams of poems of endearment
On leaves of silk from Samarkand.

There you could read with mounting pleasure
What I had ordered from Ormuz,
And how the commerce of the planet
Was set in motion just for you;

How in the country of the Brahmins
A multitude of fingers strove,
So all of Hindustan in splendour
Would bloom for you on wool and silk;

Yes, for the glory of my lover
The torrents dredged through Sambalpur,
To wash from earth, debris and rubble,
The diamonds that were meant for you;

How bands of hardy divers ravaged
The oysters' treasures from the Gulf,
That whole divans of seasoned experts
Devote themselves to grade for you.

And when at length in Basra gathered,
With spice and incense added in,
The riches that delight the nations
Are brought to you on caravans.

Yet all this bounty fit for sultans,
At last it only blinds the eyes;
For spirits genuinely loving,
Will in each other find their joy.

Would I hesitate to give you
Balkh, Bokhara, Samarkand,
Cities brimming with distractions,
Just for you, my darling one?

Now suppose you ask the Khan if
He would do the same for you?
His magnificence and wisdom
Keep him unaware of love.

Master, giving such a present
Wouldn't cross your mind at all,
Till you had a girl like this one,
And were just as poor as me!

BOOK OF SULEIKA

The fine calligraphy,
Gilded magnificence,
You favoured with smiles,
The too forward addresses;
Forgave my boasting
Of your regard, the boast that
Through you happiness was conquered,
Forgave a delicate self-praise.
Self-praise! – Only envy gags –
Perfume to friendship,
It suits our tastes!

Joy of existence is great;
Greater the joy in living
When you, Suleika,
Engulfing me with delight,
Fling your passion into my court,
Just like a ball,
Which I then hold, to
Pitch in return my
Wholly dedicate self:
There you have peaks in life!
Then they drag me away,
First the Frank, and then the Armenian.

Only after days,
After decades, can I recreate the
Wealth that you have broadcast in countless layers,
Unravel my fortune's bright-coloured cord,
A thousand fibres woven
By you, my Suleika!

Here in exchange then,
Pearls of the poet,
Those the ocean breakers threw,
Your forceful emotions
Cast on the shores of
An empty existence.
With slender fingers
Deftly selected,
Strung through and interlaced with
Gold stuff:
Place them around your throat,
Upon your bosom!
The drops of rain from Allah,
Matured by this humblest of molluscs.

Love for love and hour for hour, and
Word for word and glance for glance;
Kiss for kiss from truest lips, and
Breath for breath and joy for joy.
So at night and in the morning!
Yet you sense within my songs that
Always there's a secret anguish;
Could I borrow Joseph's looks, so
I can parallel your beauty.

BOOK OF SULEIKA

Suleika
People, slave and king together,
All agree in any age:
Highest joy of earthly beings
Rests in their identity.

Every life is worth the living
If one only keeps oneself:
We can bear with any loss as
Long as we stay what we are.

Hatem
That may be! I get the meaning,
Yet I'm on another trail:
Earthly joys I find united
Only in Suleika here.

When she squanders *her* self on me,
Then *my* self's a worthy 'I';
Should she then be turning elsewhere,
In a moment I'm no more.

Then, with Hatem, all were ended;
Yet I'd soon exchange my fate:
Swiftly I'd take on the being
Of the lover in her arms.

I'd be – well, not quite a rabbi,
That would hardly do for me –
Mutanabbi, or Ferdausi,
Caesar should the need arise.

Hatem

Like the coloured polished lights of
Goldsmiths' counters in the market,
So a set of pleasing girls are
Flocking round the greying poet.

Girls

Still you sing about Suleika!
This we'd rather not put up with;
Not for you, but for your poems,
We have reason to be jealous.

Even though she were a monster,
You'd transform her to a beauty,
Just as we have often read of
Jamil and his old Buteina.

Since it's clear that we're good-looking,
We should like our portraits painted,
And if you can do them cheaply,
We shall see you well rewarded.

Hatem

Come, the brunette, I'll enjoy it;
Braids and combs, if large or tiny,
Give a little head adornment,
Just as domes adorn a mosque.

You, the little blonde, so graceful,
All your ways so fine and dainty;
It would not seem out of order,
Minarets be likened to you.

BOOK OF SULEIKA

You behind are blest with eyeballs
Set at odds, and can employ them
Each according to your pleasure;
So it's best that I avoid you.

One, bedecked with gentle eyelid,
Shines to overwhelm the starlight,
Signifies the height of mischief,
Yet the other seems so modest.

This one, when the other injures,
Tries to nourish me and heal me,
I could not pronounce as happy
One who lacked this twin surveillance.

Thus could all receive my praises,
Thus could all receive my worship:
For as I applaud your virtues,
So my mistress too is pictured.

Girls

Poets relish their enslavement,
Since a lordship rises from it;
Yet it should seem best of all that
Your own darling be a poet.

Has she expertise at singing,
Is her voice as skilled as ours?
For it renders us suspicious
That she works in secrecy.

Hatem

Now, who knows of her achievements!
Have you met such hidden depths?
Self-engendered song is flowing,
Self-transmitted from her mouth.

Out of all you poetesses
Not a one can be her match:
While she sings to give me pleasure,
Self is all *you* love and sing.

Girls

Now it's clear that you're pretending
That a houri is your lover!
Let it be! so long as there's no
Earthly being that you flatter.

BOOK OF SULEIKA

Hatem

Tresses, hold me in subjection
In the circle of her face!
For you dark and cherished serpents
I have nought to counter with.

Heart alone retains endurance,
Proffers juvenile bouquets;
Under snow and fog and shower
Etna stokes a flame for you.

You with morning's redness make a
Greying summit blush with shame;
Yet again has Hatem felt the
Breath of spring and summer's heat.

Saki, here! Another bottle!
Here's a drink I pledge to her!
Should she find a hill of ashes,
She can say: 'He burned for me'.

Suleika*

I shall never be without you!
Love shall give to love its strength.
You can grace my youthful freshness
With your passion's seasoned force.

Ah! it flatters my emotions
When they celebrate my poet:
Since that life consists of loving,
And the life of life is spirit.

* *Written by Marianne.*

O do not let your vermilion lips
Be cursing this ill-mannered passion;
What defence has our pain of love
Unless it seek for assuagement?

Should you be cut off from one that you love,
Like Orient from Occident,
Your heart through all the deserts runs;
Your heart forever goes guide to itself;
And Baghdad's – for lovers – not far.

Let your cracked planet forever
Try to make of itself a whole!
These unclouded eyes are in lustre,
And this heart, it beats for me!

O that the senses number more than one!
Bewildering the happiness I feel:
When I observe you, wishing I were deaf,
When you are speaking, blind.

Though in the distance, you're so near!
And unexpected comes the ache.
And when afresh I hear you speak,
At once you're at my side again!

BOOK OF SULEIKA

How shall I stay contented,
Cut off from day and light?
My wish is now for writing,
I do not care for drink.

When she at first allured me,
To speak was not our way,
And as the tongue had faltered,
So falters now my pen.

Go on! beloved Saki,
In stillness fill the glass!
I only say: Remember!
It's clear then what I want.

When I dream about you,
Saki leaps to ask me:
'Master, why so still!
For you know I'm always
Keen for your instruction,
Long to hear your words.'

When the self's forgotten
Underneath the cypress,
He has no respect;
Yet in spheres of silence
I become so knowing,
Wise as Solomon.

WEST-EASTERN DIVAN

Suleika's Book

I'd dearly like to see this book more neatly gathered,
So that it's like the others better laced,
But how propose to shorten words and pages,
When lovers' madness takes us out of bounds?

On foliage-laden branches,
My darling, look above!
See how the fruits are gathered,
Enclosed in spikes and green.

For long they dangle rounded,
Close, unaware of self;
A bough, like rocking water,
Sways patient lullabies.

Still ripening from inwards,
The kernel swells and browns:
It seeks to win the breezes
And longs to see the sun.

The skin gives way, and downward
It gladly plummets free:
So tumble all my poems
In heaps upon your lap.

BOOK OF SULEIKA

Suleika
I, at happy fountains' rim,
Where they played in liquid threads,
Did not know what held me fast;
It was something from your hand,
My initials lightly outlined:
Down I glanced, at your inviting.

Here, where water ends its flow
In the tree-lined avenue,
I afresh cast eyes above,
And I see there once again,
My initials finely outlined:
Stay! O stay, at my inviting!

Hatem
May the springing, welling water
And the cypresses confess:
From Suleika to Suleika
Is my going, my return.

Suleika
Scarcely are you mine again, and
Feasted on my kisses, singing,
Than you're quiet, introspective;
What disturbs you, presses, troubles?

Hatem
O Suleika, shall I say it?
I must weep instead of praising!
Once you sang my poems only,
Ever new, repeated ever.

I should give these approbation,
Yet they come as interlopers;
Not from Hafez, or Nizami,
Not from Sadi, Jami neither.

I know well the troop of masters,
Word for word and all the music,
Firmly fixed in my remembrance;
These you sing are newly written.

They were written yesterday, so
Tell me, have you changed allegiance?
Do you, shameless, breathe against me
Inspirations of a stranger,

These to bring you equal fervour,
Equal in their soaring ardour,
Luring, calling to a union,
Just as musical as mine are?

Suleika
While Hatem was so long abroad,
The girl has added to her skills;
By Hatem she was highly praised:
The separation stood the test.
Now, so they're not called foreign poems:
They are Suleika's, therefore Hatem's!

BOOK OF SULEIKA

Bahramgur found the art of rhyming verses,
Impelled to speak by his delighted soul;
Dilaram then, his girl for loving hours,
Replied to him with matching words and sound.

And thus, my darling, you were granted to me,
To find through you the pleasant use of verse,
So I no longer have a need to envy
The Sassanid Bahramgur: now it's mine.

You woke this book in me, conferred it on me;
Since what I gladly spoke from brimming heart,
Is echoed back from your beloved being,
As glance for glance, so verse for verse returned.

It now resounds to you: through any distance
The written word, though sound be lost in space.
Is this not stars in freshly scattered mantles?
Is this not love's transfigured universe?

Taking comfort from your glances,
From your lips and from your breast,
Hearing you as you were speaking,
Was my first and last delight.

Yesterday, alas, it ended,
All the light and fire subsided;
All the games that brought me pleasure,
Changed to costly obligations.

Till it should be Allah's will,
You and I be reunited,
Sun and moon and earth are mere
Pretexts for a fit of weeping.

Suleika*

What's the meaning of these stirrings?
Does the East Wind bring good tidings?
Freshened motion of its wings shall
Cool the spirit's deepest anguish.

Play caressing with the dust and
Hunt it up in gentle cloudlets,
Drive to shelter in the vineyards
Happy tribes of little insects.

Gently soothe the glow of sunshine,
Cool as well my burning cheeks, and
In its flying, kiss the vineyards
That emblazon field and hillside.

And its gentle whispers bring a
Thousand greetings from the lover;
Well before the hill is dark, a
Thousand kisses shall salute me.

You can now be on your way! to
Serve the loving and the troubled.
Where the lofty walls are glowing,
Soon I'll find the one I cherish.

Ah, the truest lover's-tidings,
Breath of love, and life's renewal,
From his mouth alone can issue,
These alone his breathing give me.

* Written by Marianne.

BOOK OF SULEIKA

Divine Image

The sun, the Helios of pagans,
Rides splendid on celestial roads;
Assured of universal conquest,
He casts around, below, above.

He sees the fairest goddess weeping,
The vapour's daughter, heaven's child;
He seems to shine for her uniquely,
Then blind to other cheerful spots,

He sinks himself in pain and shower,
And stronger flow her streams of tears;
He broadcasts joy within her sadness
And every pearl receives a kiss.

Intense she feels the staring vigour,
And fixedly returns his glance;
The pearls desire a transformation,
For each is imaged with the sun.

And so, enwreathed in bow and colour,
A brightness radiates her face;
Towards her he is strongly driven;
She stays, alas! beyond his reach.

You, prey to cruel strokes of fortune,
Flee from me, ruining delight;
And were I Helios the Mighty,
What use to me a flying throne?

Afterthought

It rings so splendid, when the poet
Compares himself to potentates and suns;
But he conceals the spectacle of heartache,
When he goes creeping through the dark.

Encumbered by its streaks of clouding,
The heavens' purest blue declined to night;
My cheeks are ashy, pale and meagre,
And wan the tears that fill my heart.

Don't leave to me the night, the sorrow,
You All-Beloved, you my shining moon!
O you my morning star and beacon,
My sun in daybreak, you my light!

Suleika*

Ah, for moisture-laden plumage,
West Wind, how I feel an envy:
Since to him you can convey the
News of separation's torment.

It's the motion of your wings that
Wakes a yearning in the bosom,
Eyes and flowers, hill and forest
Stand in tears through your incitement.

Yet your mild and gentle breathing
Cools the eyelids from their anguish;
Ah, for sorrow must I perish,
Were I not in hope to see him.

Hurry then to my beloved,
Whisper gently to his spirit;
Yet forbear to cause him sadness,
Still conceal from him my heartache.

Tell him, but reveal it humbly:
Say his love is all my life, and
Joyfulness in love and life are
Given by his hoped-for presence.

* *Written by Marianne.*

Reunion

Can it be! The brightest star is
Grappled to my heart again!
Oh, the nights of separation,
Chasms filled with agony!
Yes, it's you, the sweet beloved
Partner for my happiness;
When I think the hurt we've suffered,
Present troubles make me blench.

When the world as deep potential
Lay in God's eternal breast,
He ordained the dawn of time in
His supreme creative joy;
He then uttered 'Let there be!'- and
Cries of torment sounded forth,
God's almighty gesture breaking
Universe from Absolute.

Light appeared, and timid darkness
Crept away to hide its face;
And at once the elements were
Fleeing from their counterparts.
Coursing brutal desert nightmares,
Each to far horizons ran,
Rigid, dead, in space unmeasured,
Lacking feeling, lacking sound.

BOOK OF SULEIKA

All was mute and still and barren –
God was struck by loneliness!
So in mercy to the anguished,
He created scarlet dawn:
Morning drew kaleidoscopes of
Sounding colours through the murk:
Entities that plunged from contact
Now could stir with love again.

Thus with agitated striving
Partners seek where they belong;
And to life without restriction
Feeling, vision, set their course:
Whether seizing, whether grasping,
If they just are holding fast!
Allah need create no further:
We create the world ourselves.

So the wings of morning passion
Tore me to your waiting kiss;
Nights of strength and starry brightness
Seal our bond a thousand times.
We together on this earth are
Paragons in joy and strife;
But a second 'Let there be!' shall
Never make us part again.

Night of Full Moon

Mistress, why the gentle whispers?
What impels your lips so lightly?
Ever sweet with murmurings,
Lovelier than sips of nectar!
Do you think to draw a kindred
Pair of lips to join your own?
   'Let me kiss and kiss, I whispered!'

See! by this uncertain darkness,
Blossom glowing on the branches,
Falling star on falling star;
Emeralds are piercing thickets,
Thousandfold a show of jewels;
Yet your heart is far away.
   'Kiss, O let me kiss, I whispered!'

Your adored, in distant places,
Tastes as well this bittersweetness,
Feels a joy in his distress.
Each at full moon sends a greeting,
Swore in holy oath remembrance:
This is now the promised time.
   'Let me kiss and kiss, I whisper!'

BOOK OF SULEIKA

Secret Writing

Concern yourselves, ye envoys,
With matter of import,
Allow your potent masters
This sharp and clear advice!
Despatch of secret ciphers
Preoccupies the world,
Till all its twists and turnings
At last are set to rights.

My sweetest mistress gave me
The cipher now in hand,
In which I take such pleasure,
Since she devised the craft;
The fullness of our loving
In blest environment,
With true and dear intentions
Connecting her and me.

Of many thousand flowers,
A variegate bouquet,
Of entities angelic
An overflowing house;
With brightest-coloured plumage,
The heavens thickly spread,
A sounding sea of poems,
With fragrance blown above.

For unimpeded striving
A doubly secret script,
That strikes like serried arrows
The targets of our life.

Now this my revelation
Is usage old and good,
So when you've understood it,
Be mute and use it too.

Reflection

A mirror that's now my possession,
Such pleasure in glancing within,
As though by a Kaiser's medals,
I'm graced in double light;
It's not for self-approval
I search within the glass:
I thrive on human exchanges,
And such are now in train.

When I stand before the mirror,
In quiet lonely house,
She peeks, before you can catch her,
The sweetheart glances out.
I turn around quick, again she
Has vanished, she I glimpsed;
I forage within my poems,
Straightway she's there anew.

I write them all the fairer,
And more to my own taste,
Spite critics and the mockers,
For day-to-day reward:

Her image gold presented,
In praise of her alone,
In arabesques of roses
And little varnished frame.

BOOK OF SULEIKA

Suleika*

Song, I feel with deep contentment
All the inward sense you bear!
Full of love, you seem to say that
I am standing at his side;

I'm forever in his thoughts and
He directs a lover's joy
Ever to the far beloved,
She who vowed a life to him.

Yes, my heart, it is the mirror
Wherein, friend, you see yourself;
This the breast where you imprinted
Kiss on kiss a lover's seal.

Sweet the verse and pure the truth that
Fetter me in sympathy!
Clarity of love incarnate,
Dressed in robes of poetry.

* *Written by Marianne.*

(Suleika)
Leave the mirror Alexander gazed in;
What's reflected? All the same:
Quiet peoples that he, like the others,
Forced to bear a shaking, on and on.
You! no further, leave the foreign journeys!
Sing to me, of whom alone you sang.
Keep in mind that I'm alive and loving,
Keep in mind you conquered me.

The world throughout is lovely in appearance,
Superlative in grace the world of poets;
From multi-coloured, bright, or grey and silver
Dominions, night and day, the lights are gleaming.
Today for me is splendour; could it linger!
I see today through love's rose-tinted glasses.

BOOK OF SULEIKA

Thou mayst assume a myriad disguises,
Thou All-Beloved One, I see it's thee;
Thou mayst in veils of magic try concealment,
Thou Omnipresent One, I see it's thee.

In pure and youthful striving of the cypress,
All-Efflorescent One, I see it's thee;
In clear and living motion of the waters,
Thou All-Enticing One, I see it's thee.

When fountains jet their water-blossoms upward,
All-Playful One, how glad I see it's thee!
When clouds are self-creating, ever-changing,
Thou All-Diverse One, still I see it's thee.

On veils that bloom as meadow-flower carpets,
All-Starred-And-Coloured One, I see it's thee;
The ivy's thousand arms are clinging, grasping,
O All-Embracing One, I know it's thee.

When morning bursts in flame upon the summits,
Thou All-Inspiring One, I welcome thee;
When heaven over me is pure and rounded,
All-Heart-Dilating One, I breathe of thee.

What I with outer, inner senses know of,
Thou All-Instructing One, I know by thee;
And when I name the hundred names of Allah,
With each there sounds an echo naming thee.

SAKI NAMEH

Book of the Cupbearer

Yes, I am also settled in the tavern,
Like any other I was hosted;
They chattered, shouted, haggled all the day,
As glum or happy as a time affords;
Myself, I sat with inner blessedness,
I thought of my beloved – how she loves?
I'm not aware: but what is troubling me!
I worship her, the way a heart allows,
That gives itself to one and hangs a slave!
And where was parchment, where a pencil set
To make the record? – So it was! just so!

I sit alone,
Where could I better be?
Drinking wine
Here by myself;
No one curbs my freedom,
My private thoughts are welcome companions.

So practised was Muley, the thief,
That he wrote a steady hand when drunk.

The Koran was eternal, unmade?
I don't ask to know!
The Koran was created, then?
I couldn't say!
That it's the Book of Books, I know,
Like a good Musulman believe.
But if it's that wine did always exist,
There I have no doubt;
Wine though created – before the angels were –

BOOK OF THE CUPBEARER

Is perhaps also no yarn.
The drinker, whatever may be the truth,
Sees much clearer the face of God.

Young and old we should all be drunk!
Youth is a drunkenness minus wine;
A wondrous virtue's present in seniors
When they are drinking back a boyhood.
Sweet life has gone to trouble bringing
Us trouble: wine's the cure for trouble.

There's no need to ask again!
Wine is sternly disallowed.
But if you must still imbibe,
Only drink the finest wine;
You would doubly be in error,
In damnation for your cellar.

When men are sober they
Delight in evil;
If men have drunk enough,
They know what's moral;
And yet excess is quick
To add its hand in:
Hafez, enlighten me
With your perceptions!

For my opinion's not
An overstatement:
The man unfit to drink
Should not be loving;
Still, drinkers need not think

They're any better:
The man unfit to love
Should not be drinking.

Suleika
Why are you so often like a fiend?

Hatem
You know, that the body's a prison cell;
The soul was betrayed, rendered a captive;
Inside is no kind of elbow room, and
Casting about to find escape, it
Learns that the prison too is shackled:
Therefore the sweetheart's doubly endangered,
That's why, so often, it's strange in behaviour.

Seeing bodies are prison cells,
Why do just the prisons experience thirst?
Souls can profess themselves well-appointed,
And cheerful, resting sane and lucid,
But then the bottles of wine are sent,
And one by one are bouncing inside.
Soul at last no longer endures it,
Breaks them in pieces against the doorposts.

BOOK OF THE CUPBEARER

To the Waiter
Don't be so rough, you animal,
Crudely setting jugs at my nostrils!
Let a nice boy serve as my waiter, or
Else fine wine is spoiled in the pouring.

To the Cupbearer
The boy that's so graceful, you step inside,
Why do you stand there in the doorway?
You be my cupbearer from now on:
Keep the wines in flavour and brightness.

The Cupbearer speaks

You, the one with darker ringlets,
Get away, you mischief-maker!
When I serve, the Master thanks me,
Kissing me upon the forehead.

As for you, I'd lay a wager,
You'd be wanting more than kisses;
Such a face and such a bosom:
Soon my friend would be exhausted.

Don't imagine you can fool me
By pretending shy retreat, for
I'll be lying in the doorway,
Wide awake if you come creeping.

They have because of our drunkenness
Arraigned us many ways,
And have on the score of drunkenness
Never found they've said enough.
It's normal for a drunkenness
To lay men out till dawn;
And yet my personal drunkenness
Hounds me the whole of the night.
For this is lovers' drunkenness,
Tormenting without stint:
From morn to night, from night to morn
It tremors in my heart,
A heart that in the drunkenness
Of singing looms and swells,
So no one's soberer drunkenness
Presumes to lift its head.
Wine, love, and music's drunkenness,
At night-time or by day,
The godliest of drunkenness,
That plagues me and delights.

You little scamp, you!
My own self-awareness
Is always a leading concern.
And so your presence, I
Find, pleases me a lot,
You favoured youngster –
Forget I'm drinking.

BOOK OF THE CUPBEARER

See what a bedlam after midnight,
The ruckus that the tavern grew to!
The host and females! Torches! Rabble!
The wealth of arguments and insults!
The shrilling flute, the roaring drum!
It made for proper chaos –
But see me, full of love and lust,
Determined to be in it.

That I don't learn from upright men
Is something all the people censure;
Yet I do well to keep away
From strife of pedagogues and preachers.

Cupbearer
Master! You make quite a picture,
Creeping out so late this morning!
Persians call it *bidamag buden*,
Franks would say that you're hungover.

Poet
Leave me now, beloved boy, for
Me the world can hold no pleasure,
Neither gloss nor scent of roses,
Nor the nightingales in concert.

Cupbearer
Just the problem I can handle,
And I think I'll fix it simply;
Here! enjoy refreshing almonds,
So the wine regains its flavour.

Then I'll take you to the terrace
For a draught of morning breezes;
While he's watching you recover,
You can give the boy some kisses.

See! the world is not a cavern,
Still enriched with nests and fledglings;
Scent of roses, oil of roses!
Nightingales, they sing as always.

That unspeakable vixen,
The double-dealer,
Life they call her,
How she has deceived me,
Just like all of the others.
First she took faith from me,
Then she took hope,
Her sights were then
Set at love, and
I ran away.
To preserve till the end
The treasure I rescued,
Wisely I shared it,
Loving Suleika and Saki.
Each of the two has
Been ardent in competition,
Aiming that dividends be higher,
Thus am I richer by far:
Again I possess faith, as
Her love is what I have faith in!
He, with drinking, allows me
Splendidly to feel the here and now –
Who needs hope in that case!

BOOK OF THE CUPBEARER

Cupbearer

You today have eaten richly,
Yet have drunken even deeper;
What you then have left uneaten,
Now is lying in a basin.

Look, there's what we call a 'cygnet',
Morsels bloated guests look out for;
This I bring to my old swan who
Boasts and brags upon the billows.

Yet we know a singing swan is
Tolling its own funeral bell, and
Any song I'd do without if
It should mean that you were dying.

Cupbearer

They announce a famous poet,
When you step before the public;
I delight to hear your singing,
Then I wait upon your silence.

But I love you all the deeper
When I souvenir your kisses;
For a word, it fades in speaking,
But a kiss my spirit shelters.

Making verse is full of meaning;
Better still is contemplation.
Sing away to other people,
Then be silent with your Saki.

Poet
Saki, here! another bottle!

Cupbearer
Master, you have drunk sufficient;
You are known for wild excesses!

Poet
Have you yet seen me disabled?

Cupbearer
Still the Prophet banned it.

Poet
                Minion!
We're alone, so I can tell you.

BOOK OF THE CUPBEARER

Cupbearer

Once it pleases you to teach me,
Questions seldom rest unanswered.

Poet

Know! We other faithful Muslims
Should be sober at our prayers:
He, in his devoted fervour,
Longs to be the only mad one.

Saki

Master, think! when you are drinking,
Casting round a fiery glow!
Drumming lightning sparks in thousands,
Unaware what they ignite.

Hypocrites I see in corners,
When you strike upon the board,
Hide behind dissembling faces,
While your heart's upon your sleeve.

Tell me how a growing youngster,
Though he's not without his faults,
Sorely lacking in the virtues,
Yet he's wiser than a man.

You know all that's in the heavens,
All that's borne upon the earth,
Yet do not conceal the tumult
That is swarming in your breast.

Hatem
Just the reason, blue-eyed boy, for
Staying always young and wise;
Poets, true, are heaven-gifted,
Yet the gift betrays their life.

Cradled first in secrecy, then
Babbling to the world at large!
Vain a poet be discreet when
Poems give the game away.

Summer Night

Poet
Now the sun has journeyed under,
Yet it glitters in the distance;
Still I wonder just how far the
Golden shimmer will continue?

Cupbearer
Master, do you wish I loiter,
Watching here at the encampment?
Once the darkness conquers daylight,
I can run to notify you.

Well I know, you love to gaze at
Depths of boundlessness above us,
While the torches in the azure
Heap their praises on each other.

And the brightest only says that:
'I am shining as intended;
If the Lord had given vigour,
You could shine with equal brightness.'

BOOK OF THE CUPBEARER

All is wonderful to God, for
He Himself is best of all, and
Therefore all the birds are sleeping
In their big and little houses.

One of them may well be perching
On the branches of the cypress,
Where the gentle wind can rock him
Till the dampened airs of morning.

That's the kind of thing you teach me,
Or a lesson of that order;
All the learning gathered from you
Cannot dwindle from my spirit.

For your sake tonight I'm crouching
Like an owl upon the terrace,
Till I see the stars have reached the
Middle point on heaven's journey.

Then upon the hour of midnight,
When you often rise too early,
What a splendid thing for us to
See a Universe of wonder.

Poet
Yes, within the fragrant garden,
Bulbul sings from night to morning:
Still, the vigil would be something
If it matched your expectations!

In this current time of Flora,
As the pagan folk would call it,
Pale Aurora, lacking husband,
Yearns for Hesperus the graceful.

Look around! she comes! so quickly!
Over broadened fields of flowers! –
Sunlight crowds itself about us,
See, the darkness loses balance.

Now on light and rosy feet the
Goddess hurries, mad to seize him –
But he ran off with the sun, and
Can't you feel her breathing passion?

Go, my favourite disciple,
Deep inside, and bolt the shutters;
She could well mistake your beauty
For a Hesperus, and steal you.

Cupbearer (drowsy)
At last you teach me, as I had hoped,
Of God's abiding presence in the elements.
You speak the words engagingly!
But dearest of all, you give me love.

Hatem
He gently sleeps, and has a right to slumber.
You kindly boy, have poured the wine for me,
From friend and teacher, willingly and freely,
So young have grasped the old man's way of thought.
But now in sweet abundance comes good health to
Flow in your body, making you anew.
I'm drinking on, but keeping quiet, quiet –
You'll cheer me if you have unbroken sleep.

MATHAL NAMEH

Book of Parables

From Heaven fell to Ocean's raging waters
A timid droplet; brutal currents struck;
Still God rewarded lowliness and faith:
The droplet grew in strength, endurance;
A calming oyster took her in.
Today, enwreathed in lasting praises,
The pearl adorns our mighty crown imperial –
With tender, blessed, shining face.

Nightingales through rain and darkness
Sing to Allah's shining heaven;
Their reward for golden singing:
Strict duress in golden bower;
Such a cage the human body;
True, the soul is close imprisoned;
Yet on gaining right remembrance,
Little soul, it sings forever.

BOOK OF PARABLES

Belief in Miracles

On breaking once an attractive bowl
I fell in desperation;
And sure my haste and clumsiness
I wished to all the devils.

I raged and stormed, then gently grieved
The sorrowful heap of fragments;
A pitying God, at once He made
It whole as ever created.

The pearl, escaped from mollusc embrace,
The fairest, high in breeding –
To jeweller, and honest man,
She said: My life is ended!

You pierce me through: my fairest self,
At once shall be demolished,
And with my sisters, each in turn,
Be fixed in ruination.

'I only think of my reward,
And you must be forgiving:
For were I not so cruel here,
How should the strand be threaded?'

I saw with wonder and delight the
Blest Koran displaying a peacock feather:
Be welcome in this holy place,
You most extolled of earthly things!
In you, as in the stars of heaven,
Is Allah's greatness proclaimed in the little,
That He, who oversees the worlds,
Has here imprinted with His eye,
And so bedecked a flimsy down,
That emulation's scarce considered
By monarchs, such is peacocks' splendour.
Enjoy your praise in modesty,
That you be worthy of the shrine.

An emperor had two officials,
One for receipts and one for disbursements;
This one gave out so liberally, the
Other knew not where to get funding.
The spending one died; the ruler hardly knew just
Who could be entrusted with the position,
And scarcely was there time to look, when
The live official was filthy rich,
Could barely move for gold incoming,
Through one single day's hold-up in spending.
At last the ruler saw it clear,
The cause of all their days of woe.
The windfall then he knew to value,
By leaving the post forever vacant.

BOOK OF PARABLES

The kettle heard the latest pot:
Just see how black your belly is!
'That only comes from kitchen use;
This way, this way, you shining fool,
Your pride will soon be humbled.
Your handles guard an untarnished face,
But don't be toffee-nosed for that,
Be looking at your bottom.'

Big and little, all mankind,
Spin themselves an appealing web,
Where they with pointy-ended fingers
All dainty in the middle hover.
And when there comes a clearing broom,
O the unprecedented wrong!
The greatest of palaces vandalized.

From Heaven downward Jesus brought
The Gospel script, eternal and fixed;
Disciples heard Him read day and night;
Divine the Word, it took effect.
He went above; it left with Him;
But they, regardless, felt its force,
And each transcribed it, step by step,
As he retained it in his mind,
Divergent. It's really not important:
Their skills were not pitched at equal levels;
Upon them nonetheless the Christians
Eke out a life till Judgement cometh.

It is good

By light of moon in Paradise,
Jehovah found in deep repose
The sleeping Adam, laid beside
Him little Eve in a matching sleep.
And now there lay, in earthly compass,
Sweetest paired thoughts of the Almighty. –
Good!! He cried of His masterwork;
Was loth to take Himself away.

No wonder we are rapt in joy,
When glance afresh encounters glance,
As if we had so far attained
To be with Him whose thought we are.
And should He call, so be it then!
If only we can stay a pair.
I keep you in these arms' confinement,
Dearest of all the thoughts of Jehovah.

PARSI NAMEH

Book of the Parsee

Legacy of Old Persian Religion

What bequest, my brothers, should he leave you,
Poor believer ready for departure,
He the novices with patience tended,
Honouring his final days with succour?

Often when we saw the king on horseback,
Gold on him and gold on all beside him,
Precious stones on him and all his nobles,
Strewn around as thick as hail in showers,

Did you never feel a pang of envy?
Was the vision not more brightly feasted
When the sun arose on wings of morning,
Lifting over Darnavend's unnumbered

Summits circles skyward? Who refrained from
Gazing on that sight? I felt, I felt a
Thousand times, a thousand living mornings,
Flown above, with rising sun transported,

Brought to look on God enthroned in glory,
Him as Lord and Source of Life proclaiming,
Worthy then to see the highest vision,
Fit to walk in His illumination.

When the sun however finished rising,
I was blinded then and stood in darkness,
Beat my breast, and threw my wakened body
Downward, forehead first, and lay prostrated.

BOOK OF THE PARSEE

Let me testify to my convictions
In desire of brotherly remembrance:
For protection shoulder daily duties,
There's no other revelation needed.

When a newborn's gentle hands are quickened,
So that he at once is sun-directed,
Bathe his body, spirit, swift in brightness!
He shall know the grace of every dawning.

See the dead committed to the living,
Only beasts entombed in earth and rubble,
And, so far as hand and strength enable,
What you judge impure, let it be covered.

Cultivate your fields to cleanly neatness,
Let the sun in gladness shine on labour;
Set in rows the trees that you are planting,
For the sun enriches what is ordered.

Water too that's flowing in the channels
Should not lack for impetus and cleanness;
Zandarud, arising pure from mountains,
May he end his journey unpolluted.

So the fall of water's not impeded,
Set about to excavate the trenches;
Rushes, reeds, and noxious salamanders,
Misbegotten, root them out together!

When your land and water's rendered wholesome,
Then the sun delights to shine in vapours
Where it, through such laudable reception,
Fosters life, a life that's sound and upright.

You, oppressed by trial after trial,
Be consoled! for all is pure and cleanly;
Now, emboldened, men appear as priests and
Strike off from a flint the hallowed symbol.

Where the flame's ablaze, avow with gladness:
Night is bright, the limbs are warm and supple.
At the hearth's enlivened strength and vigour
Sap of beast and plant are made nutritious.

Bearing wood along, be struck with wonder,
For you carry seeds of earthly sunlight;
Picking cotton, say in gentle chorus:
This, as wick, becomes the Holy's vehicle.

Should you, godly, recognize in all the
Burning lamps a higher light's reflection,
No misfortune rises to prevent you
Worshipping at dawn the Throne of Glory.

There is kingly seal of our existence,
Mirror showing God to men and angels;
There the stammered praises of the Highest
Join together, circle after circle.

Now forsaking Zandarud's embankments,
Over Darnavend I beat my wings, till
Sunrise comes, which I shall meet with gladness,
From that place forever send you blessings.

BOOK OF THE PARSEE

When a man acclaims creation,
While the sun is warm and gleaming,
Takes his pleasure in the vine that's
Weeping under sharpened cutters –
It's aware its ripened juices,
Well fermented, wake the world, and
Render many powers active,
Many more however stifled –
Then he knows to thank the sunlight
That allows the earth to flourish;
While the drunkard staggers, stammers,
Temperate, he sings contented.

CHULD NAMEH

Book of Paradise

Foretaste

Of Paradise the Muslim makes pronouncements,
As though he drew on personal researches;
He trusts the blest Koran's unswerving promise
That pure and clear instruction here is grounded.

And yet the Prophet, maker of this volume,
He knows to scent our failings from his eyrie,
And sees, despite the thunder of his curses,
The frequent doubt that poisons our believing.

He therefore sends from realms of the eternal
A paragon of youth to bring renascence;
She flutters down, and has no hesitation
In binding round my neck a sweet entrapment.

Upon my lap, against my breast, I grasp the
Angelic soul, and wish no greater knowledge;
I now believe in Paradise with fervour,
In zealous hope of kissing her forever.

BOOK OF PARADISE

Justified Men
(after the Battle of Badr, under a heaven of stars)

Muhammad speaks

Let the foe bewail their dead companions,
Since they lie without a hope of rescue;
You should not regret *our* fallen brothers,
Out beyond the spheres they make their journey.

All the seven planets make them welcome,
Open wide their vast metallic doors;
Soon the bold transfigured men we cherish
Knock upon the Gates of Paradise.

Overjoyed, they find, beyond their wishes,
Splendours such as I descried in flight,
When the wonderhorse in just an instant
Bore me through the heavens' full expanse.

Tree on tree of wisdom, tall as cypress,
Raise their crown of golden apples high,
Trees of life, projecting spacious shadows,
Shelter lavish beds of bloom and herb.

Now the sweetest eastern breeze delivers
Regiments of girls of Paradise;
With the eyes you gain a taste of wonder,
Just a glimpse can satisfy desire.

Searchingly they quiz your earthly record:
Mighty projects? struggles laced with blood?
That you're heroes's known by your arrival;
What the breed of hero? they would know.

Soon they see the wounds upon your bodies,
These alone inscribe your deeds of fame.
Fortune, kingship, all are evanescent,
Only wounds of faith have lasting worth.

Leading you to kiosks and pavilions,
Rich with columns, coloured, crystalline,
Then to grapes' transfigured noble juices,
Friendly, they invite you with a sip.

Lads! as more than lads we give you welcome!
All the girls are equal, blithe and free;
Should you give your heart to one, however,
She is friend and mistress to your troop.

Yet the perfect being does not gather
Any hint of pleasure from your praises:
Tranquil, gracious, honest, she regales you
With the many virtues found in other maidens.

One will lead you to another's banquet,
Each excels at laying banquets out.
You have many women yet have concord,
Paradise for this alone's a worthy prize.

Therefore rest yourself in this contentment,
Since you can no longer change your fortune;
Such a girl will not exhaust your vigour,
Such a wine will not inebriate you.

Thus I speak a little of the wonders
That a blessed Musulman can boast of:
Paradise of Islam's manly heroes
Here is set in order and perfected.

BOOK OF PARADISE

Chosen Women

Women should not be the losers,
Hope resides in their devotion;
Yet we know of only four that
Dwell without a doubt in Heaven.

First Suleika, star of being,
All desire she was for Joseph,
Now, delight of Paradise, and
Flower of renunciation.

Then the Holy Blessed Virgin,
Who to heathens bore salvation,
And betrayed, in bitter sorrow,
Saw Him led to crucifixion.

Next Muhammad's wife, who built his
Fortune and his glory, whilst she
Urged monogamy, and likewise
Fostered monotheist doctrine.

Lastly Fatima, the blessed,
Daughter, wife of true perfection,
Soul of pure angelic nature
Borne in flesh of gold and honey.

These we find installed in Heaven;
Any man who values women,
He deserves to walk with these in
Pleasant journeys through hereafter.

Admittance

Houri
I today am keeping watch in
Front of Paradise's Gate,
Now uncertain what to do, as
You have such a suspect look!

Whether you have truly been a
Muslim faithful to our kind?
Did your battles or your merit
Send you here to Paradise?

Do you count yourself a hero?
Please display a hero's wounds;
Should the record be praiseworthy,
I shall usher you inside.

Poet
Don't be so punctilious, and
Let me in without ado!
As a man I lived a life, and
So that means I fought a fight.

Sharpen up your searching glances!
Give attention to this breast,
See the marks of life's unkindness,
See the marks of cruel desire!

Yet I sang believers' songs that
Said my love was true to me,
Said the world, however turning,
Stays a loving, grateful world.

And I strove for excellence, and
Reached to such a pitch of skill,
Now my name in flames of love is
Blazoned on the finest hearts.

No! you choose no petty being!
Give your hand, that day by day
I upon your tender fingers
Count away eternity.

Approval

Houri
Out at that station
Where I spoke to you first,
Keeping watch at the gateway,
Frequently my task,
I heard there astonishing disturbance,
A noise of syllables rustling,
And aiming within;
No one showed their face however,
Then it faded till it died;
It sounded though just like Darling's poems –
Yet again I recall it.

Poet
Ever-Beloved! what kind
Remembrance you have of your sweetheart!
Whatever else of terrestrial make
Can pass as poems,
They all aspire to be here:
Many are calling, down there in their droves;

Others that the spirit animates,
Like the flying horse of Muhammad,
Levitate up and whistle
Out there at the gate.
And happen your comrades should meet with such,
They ought to pay friendly attention,
And kindly amplify echoes,
So they travel resounding downward;
And ought to take trouble,
When it does occur the
Poet comes, that his gifts are
Met with the best requitals;
Thus do good in two dimensions.

They ought to reward him kindly,
In lovable ways compliant,
And vouchsafe him lodging with them:
Worthy fellows aren't demanding.

You though are my portion only,
I won't grant you leave from peace that's eternal;
Keeping watch is not your task now,
Send out a girl who is lacking for work!

Poet
Your devotion, your kiss bring me joy!
I would not be trespassing on secrets;
But tell me, if you have never partaken of
Temporal existence?
It's often forced on my awareness,
It's something I'd swear to, I'd like to confirm it:
That once you bore the name of Suleika.

Houri

From primary elements we were fashioned,
From water, fire, and earth and air,
Unmixed and pure; terrestrial taints
Are quite discrepant with our natures.
We don't descend to your condition;
And when you come to dwell with us,
You give us quite enough to do.

For, you see, when believers approached us,
Sent with the Prophet's own commendation,
And laying claim to Paradise, O
There we all were, as he had ordered,
So full of kindness, rich with charm
As even angels had never known.

And yet they, one and then another,
We found they had a special girl already –
Frightful things should you set them against us –
Yet they considered us quite inferior;
Though we were charming, clever, cheerful,
The Muslims pined for earthly existence.

To us of heaven's gentle breeding
Behaviour such as this was horrid,
And so we devious intriguers
Engaged in a lengthy collusion;
And when Muhammad flew through Paradise,
We figured out his chosen path;
As he was carelessly heading home
We seized the flying horse's reins.

But did we hold him at our mercy? –
Firm but fair, best Prophetic manner –
Brusquely he circulates us with orders;
We though were very much incommoded,
Since he, to carry out his purpose,
Left us alone to shoulder burdens;
As you suspected, this was our mission,
We should resemble all your girlfriends.

All of our self-importance went for nothing,
We ladies scratched our heads in amazement,
Yet, so we thought, in life everlasting
We must submit to the things that are sent us.

Now each man sees as he once saw,
And what occurred, occurs again.
We are the blondes and we are the dark ones,
We have the moods and all those caprices,
Yes, sometimes even such palaver,
A fellow thinks himself remarried;
And we moreover are gleeful that men
Can imagine it's really so.

You though possess a freer temper,
To you I am truly heavenly;
You honour glances, honour kisses,
And would if I should not be Suleika.
And since she was so lovable,
I look like her right to a tee.

BOOK OF PARADISE

Poet

You dazzle me with Heaven's brightness,
Though it be truth or just imposture,
Enough, I am fixed in admiration.
To briskly carry out her duty,
And bring a pleasure to a German,
Here is a houri that prattles verses.

Houri

And you can rhyme away unstinted,
Just as it springs up from your heart!
The fellowship of the immortals
Inclines to best intents in words and deeds.
The beasts, as you know, will not be excluded,
If they're obedient, show themselves as true!
A houri's not put off by lack of polish;
We feel what's spoken from the soul,
And what has leapt from purest springs
May flow in Paradise unhindered.

Houri

Tapping me upon the shoulder once more:
Do you know, how many aeons
We have dwelt lovingly together?

Poet

No! – And will not know it. No!
Pleasures various, ever renewed,
Ever chaste and bridal kiss! –
When every moment deluges through me,
Why should I question, how long it may linger!

Houri

I know there yet were times once before,
When you were rapt, knew unbounded life.
Faith in the cosmos you sustained,
With heart to sound the depths of God;
Now to your darling give attention!
Have you the little poem ready?
How did they clamour at the gate?
And now? – I shan't go piling on the pressure,
Sing me the songs that your Suleika heard:
You won't do better poems, even here in Heaven.

Favoured Animals

Four beasts were also given pledge
They'd enter into Heaven,
And there forever make their home
With sanctified believers.

An ass is granted precedence,
His gait is light and cheerful:
He carried to Jerusalem
Our blessed prophet Jesus.

Half bashful comes the wolf that took
This order from Muhammad:
'Forbear to steal the poor man's sheep,
The wealthy you may plunder.'

His tail a-wagging, blithesome, brave,
With his courageous master,
That faithful little dog who joined
In sleep with seven sleepers.

Abuharrira's cat is here,
Growls at his lord and wheedles:
And any beast the Prophet stroked
Will stay a sainted creature.

Higher and Highest

That we preach of such a matter
Need not earn us castigation:
Full awareness charges you to
Sound the oceans of your nature.

Then you reach this understanding:
Men, complacent, wish to see the
Preservation of their ego,
As on Earth so there in Heaven.

And my favoured 'I' enjoins a
Quantity of lazy comforts;
Pleasures such as I have fed on,
I should like forever after.

So we're pleased by lovely gardens,
Flowers, fruit, and pretty children,
All that here affords delight to
Suit no less a soul refashioned.

Thus I want my dear companions,
Young and old, together gathered,
Quite content in German words to
Stammer at a heaven's language.

Yet we hear the dialects that
Men and angels get to sample,
Exercising secret grammars
Known to poppies and to roses.

Then we like the new indulgence
Of a rhetoric of glances,
Raised without the help of hearing
To celestial enjoyments.

Understandably our speech is
Keen to rid itself of sound as
Our transfiguration leads to
Firmer grasp of boundless being.

Thus it is with all the senses,
Paradise has made provision,
Sure it is that I attain a
Single sense to serve their purpose.

Then I fly throughout the cosmos,
Buoyant where the spheres eternal
Carry deep vibrating themes of
God's transparent living music.

Soaring unrestricted, burning,
There's no ending to discover,
Till the face of Love Abiding
Draws us upward, and we vanish.

Seven Sleepers

Six, beloved of the palace,
Flee before the Caesar's anger,
Who, a god, accepted worship,
Yet whose bearing was not godlike:
Since a fly impeded Caesar
From enjoying dainty morsels.
His attendants fan and worry,
Yet cannot deter the insect.
It besieges, stings, confounds him,
Disconcerts the whole assemblage,
Keeps returning like the Lord of
Flies' malignant emissary.

'Now' – the lads confer together –
'Shall a fly impede immortals?
Shall a god be drinking, feeding
Like us humans? No, the Godhead
Who created sun and moon, and
Made the glowing dome of starlight,
He is God, let's run!' A shepherd
Led away the finely clothed and
Lightly sandalled lads, concealed them
With himself in rocky cavern.
Shepherd's dog, persistent escort,
Shooed away, a foot disabled,
Drags himself towards his master,
Takes his place beside the hidden,
Joins the ones that sleep has favoured.

And the prince that they were fleeing,
Spurned, indignant, thinks to punish,
Yet avoids the sword or burning,
Sees them walled up in the cavern,
Seals them in with brick and plaster.

But they each continue sleeping,
And the angel, their protector,
Says, reporting to the Godhead,
I to right and left forever
Keep them turning, ever turning,
Thus the young and charming bodies
Suffer no decay or moulder.
Rocks I split apart in fissures,
So the sun in rising, sinking,
Fresh renews the youngsters' faces:
Thus they lie enclosed in blessings,
While, his paw regenerate, the
Puppy sleeps in sweetest slumber.

Years are passing, years are flying,
Till at last the lads awaken,
And with age the wall has rotted,
In decrepitude has tumbled.
Then Iamblika says, the handsome,
More accomplished than the others,
While the timid shepherd wavers:
'I shall run! and bring refreshment,
Venture life and gold together!'

Ephesus, for many years now,
Hallows teachings of the prophet
Jesus. (Peace be on Him always!)

So he ran. But all is altered,
Gateway, wall and looming tower.
Still he found the nearest baker,
Hasty in his search for rations.
'Rogue!' exclaimed the baker, 'have you,
Youngster, found a hidden treasure!
Give me, since the gold betrays you,
Half the treasure for my silence!'

So they wrangle. To the ruler
Comes the quarrel; and the ruler
Wants a portion like the baker.

Now a prodigy is published
By a hundred advertisements.
In the palace he constructed
He is sure to prove his title.
Then a pillar, excavated,
Leads to nominated treasures.
His descendants quickly gather,
With the aim of showing kinship.
While Iamblika, youth in flower,
Stands a splendid distant forebear.
Hears a son or grandson named as
If an ancient predecessor;
His descendants band around him,
Men courageous, like a nation,
Him to honour, that was youngest!
Then another sign has clinched it,

Now imposed a final judgement;
For himself and for his comrades,
Their identity established.

Now returning to the cavern,
His companions king and people. –
Yet to people, nor to king does
He return, the one who's Chosen:
As the seven, who for lifetimes
Now were cut off from existence –
Eight if you append the canine –
Gabriel's unseen exertions
See them, heeding God's commandment,
Safe conducted into Heaven,
While the cavern shows no entrance.

Good Night!

Go to rest now, darling poems,
In the bosom of my people!
While within a cloud of musk the
Angel Gabriel is pleased to
Guard the weary poet's body,
Till he fresh and well in order,
Blithe as ever, loving friendship,
Breaches rocky barriers, reaches
Open plains of Paradise, and
With the heroes of all ages,
Takes his fill of all enjoyments;
Where the beautiful and young are
Ever springing on each side and
Bringing pleasure to the hosts; and
Yes, the puppy too, the faithful,
May accompany the Masters.

A selection from the
unpublished poems

Black the shadow that steps on the dust –
My beloved's companion;
Myself to dust am humbled –
Still does the shadow step over, walk on.

Why can't I employ a symbol
As I would prefer?
Since to symbolize our being,
God has picked a gnat.

Why can't I employ a symbol
As I would prefer?
In my lover's eyes the Lord has
Symbolized Himself.

A SELECTION FROM THE UNPUBLISHED POEMS

To Hafez

Hafez, to presume to match you?
How absurd!
Borne aloft by ocean swells, a
Vessel rushes on,
Feels the wind inflate the canvas,
Cruises brave and proud;
Though the sea invoke destruction,
Fragile timbers hold.
In your singing, light and rapid,
Freshened currents rise,
Boiling up to glowing waves of
Flame, and swamping me.
Still, there's one conceit tumescent
In my upstart soul:
I, like you, in bright and sunny
Lands have lived and loved!

Hudhud spoke: 'With just a glance she
Has confided all to me.
And I stand by your good fortune
As exalted as before.

'Love her then! – In nights apart see
How it's written in the stars:
Blending with eternal powers,
Glittering your love abides.'

Hudhud hiding in a palm tree,
In a bolt-hole,
Nestling, ogling, he's so cute!
And he's ever vigilant.

Conformity, correction, deformation,
For fifty years they've tried to push them on you;
But still I thought that you would best discover,
Within your native land, your best potential.
You had a time of lawlessness, with wild and
Devilish, inspirited crews of young ones;
Then slowly you have grown, as years are passing,
The nearer to the gentle, wise, and godlike.

Speak! under which of Heaven's signs is
The day set
When my heart, that's still my own, will
Fly off no more?
And, when it flies, it finds its target
Lies close to me?
On the pillow, the sweet, and the gentle,
Where my heart and hers are lain.

A SELECTION FROM THE UNPUBLISHED POEMS

Splendid you are like musk, and
Where you were, you still hold our sense.

Let me weep then! confined in night,
In a measureless desert.
The camels rest, asleep are the drivers,
Counting out wealth the Armenian;
A little way aside, I reckon the miles that
Keep me from Suleika, endlessly rehearsing
The trail's overlengthening, maddening meanderings.

Let me weep then! not a thing that's shameful:
Men while they weep are good men.
Thus did Achilles lament his Briseis!
Xerxes lamented the multitude that was doomed;
For the boyfriend he'd murdered in fury,
Alexander sorrowed.
Let me weep then! Tears to awaken the dust,
To green it.

And why not sending,
My captain-horseman,
Not sending couriers
In daily relays?
He has the horses,
He knows the script.

He knows the writing,
Can do it neatly,
Talik or Neski
On silken pages.
To stand for him then,
Give me a word.

This sufferer will not,
Will not be cured of
Her sweetest sickness,
She, by the news of
Her lover's wellness
Is rendered sick.

Writing in Neski,
He says it truly,
Writing in Talik,
It's just as welcome,
One or the other,
Enough! he loves.

A SELECTION FROM THE UNPUBLISHED POEMS

No more on silken leaves
Writing symmetrical verses;
No more binding them
With golden ribbons;
I write on the dust, in its endless motion,
Blown across by the wind; yet the effect endures,
Reaching earth's extremest centre,
The ground is held in spell.
And the nomad approaches,
The lover. When he reaches
These environs, he's struck
Throughout his being.
'Here! before me, was a lover, but
Was it Majnun the tender?
Farhad the powerful? Jamil the trustworthy?
Was it some other one of
Blessed-unfortunate thousands?
He loved! I love in my turn,
I sense him!'
Suleika, you though at rest
On the gentle cushion
That I have prepared, adorned for you,
You as well it strikes throughout your being.
'It's Hatem who cries, Hatem.
And I cry to you, O Hatem, Hatem!'

GLOSSARY

Abbas	A great Shah of Persia.
Abraxas	A mysterious cabbalistic or gnostic symbol.
Abuharrira	A friend of Muhammad.
Achilles	A Greek hero of the Trojan War who brooded when Agamemnon took away his lover Briseis.
Adam	The first man – in the Jewish, Christian, and Muslim traditions.
Alexander	Macedonian conqueror, of Persia and much else besides. His mirror displayed the world. He killed his friend Cleitus when drunk.
Allah	The God of Islam.
Anwari	Persian poet.
Arafat	A sacred hill near Mecca.
Armenian	A people renowned for commerce.
Asra	See 'Wamik'.
Aurora	Roman goddess of the dawn.
Badakshan	A region in what is now northern Afghanistan.
Badr	A battle critical in the establishment of Muhammad's power.
Baghdad	A great city on the Tigris. For several centuries one of the world's chief centres of culture.
Bahramgur	Persian ruler of the Sassanian period. Said to have invented rhymed verse.
Balkh	A city of Central Asia.
Basra	A trading city of Mesopotamia, near the Persian Gulf.

Bokhara	A city of Central Asia.
Brahmin	Archaic term for a Hindu.
Briseis	The captive girl who was a lover of Achilles.
Bulbul	The nightingale (*qv*).
Buteina	She and Jamil were passionately in love until old age.
Caesar	Title for a Roman Emperor.
Calderon	A Spanish author.
Cloth of Cloths	Saint Veronica took the likeness of Jesus upon a cloth when she wiped his face as he walked to crucifixion.
Cupbearer	A stock figure in Persian poetry, known as Saki. The boy who pours wine for the poet, and receives his praises.
Cupid	Roman god of love.
Cypress	In Persian poetry, a common image for the beloved.
Damascus	A city in Syria.
Darnavend	A mountain in Persia.
Dilaram	A mistress of Bahramgur (*qv*), associated with him in the invention of rhyming verse.
Divan	A collection of poems by one author. Can also mean a panel of experts.
Doge	Elected ruler of Venice. Annually he wed the sea.
Ebusuud	A mufti of Istanbul who pronounced upon Hafez' poems.
Elohim	A name of God in the Old Testament.
Ephesus	A Greek city in what is now western Turkey.

GLOSSARY

Etna	A volcano in Sicily.
Euphrates	With the Tigris, the major river of Mesopotamia.
Eve	The first woman. Formed from Adam's rib.
Farhad	In love with Shirin, but kept from her, he committed suicide when falsely told of her death.
Fatima	Daughter of Muhammad and wife of Ali, who was the fourth Caliph of Islam.
Fatwa	A pronouncement by an Islamic lawgiver.
Ferdausi	Epic poet of Persia.
Flora	The Roman goddess of flowers.
Frank	Common Eastern term for a European.
Gabriel	An archangel.
Ginkgo Biloba	A tree from the Far East, characterized by leaves that appear to be two fused together as one.
Gulf	The Persian Gulf.
Hafez	Muhammad Shamsuddin, the fourteenth-century Persian poet who helped inspire Goethe to write the *Divan*. He was named Hafez ('Rememberer') because he knew the Koran by heart. Rumours of his private life troubled the faithful, as with Goethe.
Hatem	An ageing poet, here representing Goethe.
Hatem Tai	An Arab poet renowned for his generosity.
Hatem Tograi	A Persian poet.
Hegira	A flight, the most notable instance being the escape of Muhammad from Mecca to Medina, the event from which the Muslim era is dated.

Helios	The sun god of the Greeks.
Hesperus	The evening star.
Hindustan	An old name for India.
Houri	The houris are the beautiful women of the Muslim paradise, who cater to a man's every need.
Hudhud	The hoopoe bird. Sent to the Queen of Sheba by King Solomon, who understood the language of birds.
Hutten, Ulrich	Controversial German poet of the time of the Reformation.
Islam	Means 'submission to God'. And a religion that stresses the oneness of God.
Jalaluddin Rumi	Persian poet.
Jami	Persian poet.
Jamil	See 'Buteina'.
Jehovah	The God of the Old Testament.
Jesus	The Messiah of the Christians, he is revered by the Muslims as a prophet.
Joseph	The pattern of male beauty. In the Islamic tradition, he was the beloved of Suleika (*qv*).
Kaiser	German term for an emperor.
Khizer	A figure of Middle Eastern mythology, who found the Water of Eternal Life. His name means 'the Green Man'.
Koran	The Holy Book of Islam. There was dispute as to whether the Koran was created by Allah or, like Him, had always existed.
Layla	In love with Majnun (*qv*), she refused to consummate her marriage to another man.

GLOSSARY

Lokman	A legendary wise man of ancient Arabia, physically ugly.
Lord of Flies	Beelzebub, the Devil.
Mahmud	Sultan of Ghazni. For many poets, a paragon among rulers.
Majnun	A legendary lover of unswerving fidelity. Kept away from Layla (*qv*), he lived in the desert with wild animals, and composed verses. 'Majnun' was actually a nickname, meaning 'madman': his real name was Kais.
Mars	The Roman god of war, and a planet with a dangerous aspect in astrology.
Mecca	The most holy city of Islam, and chief goal of pilgrimage.
Mizri	A Turkish poet.
Mufti	A lawgiver in Islam.
Muhammad	The founder of Islam. He rode to Heaven on a flying horse. His first wife was Khadija and, while she lived, he did not practise polygamy.
Musulman	Archaic term for a Muslim.
Mutanabbi	A great Arab poet.
Neski	A style of calligraphy.
Nightingale	Symbol of the lover in Persian poetry. In love with the rose.
Nizami	A Persian poet.
Noah	The inventor of wine, and the first man to get drunk.
Ormuz	A trading city in the Persian Gulf.
Oxus	A river of Central Asia. One of the barriers between the 'civilized' world of Persia and the 'barbaric' world of Central Asia.

Pand	A 'Book of Counsels' by the Persian writer Attar.
Paradise	Heaven. Also the Garden of Eden. From a Persian word meaning an enclosed park or garden.
Parsee	A practitioner of Zoroastrianism, the dominant religion of Persia before Islam. The Zoroastrians revere light and fire as symbols of the divine, and expose their dead for carrion birds. Unlike the orthodox Muslims, they favour the drinking of wine.
Persia	Nowadays known as Iran. The borders and territories of the Persian people have varied greatly during more than 2,500 years, and their cultural influence has been enormous.
Phoebus	The sun god in the Greek and Roman tradition.
Prophet	A title of Muhammad, the founder of Islam.
Rabbi	A teacher of Judaism.
Rose	Symbol of the beloved in Persian poetry. Loved by the nightingale.
Rustam	A legendary warrior hero of ancient Persia.
Sadi	Persian poet.
Saint George	One of the most widely venerated of the Christian saints, and himself a warrior, he inspired an order of knights.
Saki	The name of the cupbearer (*qv*) in Persian poetry.
Samarkand	A city of Central Asia.
Sambalpur	Locality in India.
Saturn	A planet of baleful astrological influence.

GLOSSARY

Seven Sleepers	Christians who fled the persecution of a Roman Emperor and slept in a cave for two centuries. The story was adopted by the Muslims.
Shah	Title of a Persian Emperor.
Shah Sadshan	A royal patron of Hafez. Standing for Duke Karl August of Weimar, Goethe's patron, employer, and friend.
Sheba	The Queen of Sheba was a legendary lover of King Solomon.
Shihabuddin	Struck by doubt during a pilgrimage to Mecca, he instantly received divine assurance, and donned the pilgrim's garb.
Shiraz	The beautiful Persian city where Hafez lived.
Shirin	Married to a Persian emperor, although she loved Farhad (*qv*).
Solomon	Fabled King of Israel, renowned for his wisdom.
Suleika	The wife of Potiphar who, according to the Old Testament (where she is not named), tried unsuccessfully to seduce Joseph (*qv*). In the Islamic tradition she is named and Joseph returns her love. Through love of Joseph she learns the love of God. Here Suleika represents Marianne von Willemer.
Sultan	Title of a Muslim ruler.
Talik	A style of calligraphy.
Tamina	She fell in love with Rustam (*qv*) through hearing him praised, but without having seen him.
Timur	A fourteenth-century conqueror of great power and cruelty, here representing Napoleon. Hafez was alleged to have met

	Timur, and Goethe certainly met Napoleon. Timur's failed campaign against China was matched by Napoleon's against Russia.
Vizier	Minister of an Islamic ruler.
Wamik	Although the manuscripts recounting the love of Wamik and Asra were destroyed by religious fanatics, and the details of their story were forgotten, their love remained a by-word.
Xerxes	A ruler of ancient Persia who, when reviewing a vast army, wept at the realization that everyone he saw would be dead within a hundred years.
Zandarud	A river flowing through the city of Isfahan in Persia.

Wakefield Press is an independent publishing and
distribution company based in Adelaide, South Australia.
We love good stories and publish beautiful books.
To see our full range of books, please visit our website at
www.wakefieldpress.com.au
where all titles are available for purchase.

Find us!

Twitter: www.twitter.com/wakefieldpress
Facebook: www.facebook.com/wakefield.press
Instagram: instagram.com/wakefieldpress

www.ingramcontent.com/pod-product-compliance
Lightning Source LLC
Chambersburg PA
CBHW060835190426
43197CB00040B/2613